WORLD PRAYER

Effective Prayer by J Oswald Sanders
The Prayer of Faith by J O Fraser
Prayer Tools by Will Bruce
plus devotional insights from Hudson Taylor

**30 Days of Morning and Evening
Devotional Readings on Prayer**

AN OMF BOOK

WORLD PRAYER

First published 1999
Second edition 2000
This printing 2004

OMF Books ISBN 981-3009-07-1

OMF Books are distributed by:
OMF (U.S.), 10 West Dry Creek Circle, Littleton, CO 80120
OMF (Canada), 5155 Spectrum Way, Bldg. 21, Mississauga, ON
L4W 5A1
OMF (UK), Station Approach, Borough Green, Sevenoaks, Kent
TN15 8BG
and other OMF offices.

Contents

How to contact us

To learn how you can be involved in prayer for the nations, contact your nearest OMF office at the address below:

USA   10 W. Dry Creek Circle
Littleton, CO 80120
800-422-5330

Canada   5155 Spectrum Way, Bldg. 21
Mississauga, ON L4W 5A1
905-568-9971

Britain   Station Approach, Borough Green
Sevenoaks, Kent TN15 8BG
44(1732)88-7299

Australia   PO Box 849, Epping, NSW 2121
61(2)9868-4777

Asia   2 Cluny Road, Singapore 259570
Republic of Singapore
65(475)4592

Or visit our website at www.omf.org

Editor's Foreword

This book combines the writings of four mighty men of God. Each shares insights from a life given to prayer and each reveals a heart for the lost. In order to make this already popular book more widely useful, it has been rearranged to make it possible to use it as a devotional. There are now 60 sections (30 days of morning and evening devotional readings). Since Hudson Taylor's writings were already in devotional format, they have been dispersed throughout the book, one brief devotional at the end of each section. Besides using Hudson Taylor's *When You Pray* devotional, we have also been able to add portions from five other of his works, *Dwelling In Him, Fruit Bearing, God's Fellow Workers*, God's *Guiding Hand* and *Great Is Thy Faithfulness*.

In order to keep this book helpful for those who do not want to use it as a devotional, the three sections by Sanders, Fraser and Bruce have been kept in their original order. I believe this is the best possible order as it moves the reader from Insight (Sanders) to Experience (Fraser) to Application (Bruce).

Whether you decide to use this as a devotional or just read it through as you would any book, I believe you will want to keep it on hand with your Bible after you are done and use it for years to come.

THE EDITOR

Foreword

Prayer puzzles most of us. We find it very difficult to define. Stop and think for a moment how you would define it, and you will see how hard it is. Part of the mystery is that God is neither ignorant, unwilling nor impotent, and therefore He does not need us to intercede on behalf of other men. He knows not only their needs, but also what is best for them. Yet at the same time He teaches us to pray.

The popular idea of prayer is that it is a means of making God do what we want done. This may be a crude and somewhat pagan concept, but it is by no means dead in Christian circles. The natural man has an inbuilt understanding of God, and his concept of prayer is based on the thought of God being hostile or friendly according to how He is treated. If man fulfills certain conditions, he expects God to treat him in a friendly way and to conform his circumstances or those of others to his own desires. Man's nature is basically unchanged: it centers everything around himself. The fact that prayer is a spiritual exercise by no means excludes self-interest and self-centeredness. What we want done may even be what we conceive to be God's work, and yet it may still be based on our desires rather on His will. Self-centeredness dies hard.

As I have studied the nature of prayer in the New Testament, it seems to me that there are two related aspects of it which affect each other very much. First of all comes prayer that is related to our own concept and personal relationship to God. Worship, adoration, praise, confession and communion all come under this heading. For instance, our worship and the form it takes depend very much on what we think of God and how we are related to Him. The second aspect is related to getting something done that affects our circumstances or the lives and circumstances of others. Supplication and thanksgiving come under this heading. The whole purpose of supplication, from our point of view, is that God might so intervene, as either to alter circum-

Let us not reverse the Lord's order—"first bind ... then spoil"—and still expect to effect the rescue without neutralizing the Adversary. Let us confidently accept our divine-given authority and exercise it. "Behold I have given you authority ... over all the power of the enemy" (Luke 10:19, *RSV*). Of what value is this delegation of authority if the authority is not exercised?

"Satan dreads nothing but prayer," wrote Samuel Chadwick. "His one concern is to keep the saints from praying. He fears nothing from prayerless studies, prayerless work, prayerless religion. He laughs at our toil, mocks our wisdom, but trembles when we pray."

In the history of the Overseas Missionary Fellowship, the tide in many a crisis has turned when its workers have met the situation with prayer and fasting. Many a stubborn city has opened, many an intransigent heart has yielded, many a financial need has been supplied and many a delicate personnel difficulty has been resolved by this means. While fasting is always optional in the New Testament, the record indicates that it was resorted to in the face of special temptation (Matt. 4:2); where there was a yearning after a closer walk with God (1 Cor. 7:5); where there was deep concern for evangelizing the regions beyond (Acts 13:1-3); where there was spiritual travail for the development of a church (Acts 14:21-23); where some stubborn situation had yielded to no other method (Matt. 17:21). There is still a place for prayer and fasting, though not on legalistic grounds.

The thumbnail studies in this booklet suggest some of the principles underlying effective prayer, and illustrate these principles from the lives of praying men and women of Bible times. They are presented in this form in the hope that they may prove meaningful and helpful in the hour of prayer.

OSWALD SANDERS

Creative Praying

God ... calls into existence the things that do not exist.
Have the faith of God. Romans 4:17, Mark 11:22

It appears that God acted on the principle of faith in the creation of the world. When He said to non-existent light, "Let there be light," there was light. It is this same kind of creative faith we are called on to exercise, the very faith of God. "Now faith means ... being certain of things we cannot see" (Heb. 11:1, *Phillips*), and this conception opens to us a limited realm of possibility.

The noted scientist Dr. Alexis Carrel writes: "Prayer is a force as real as terrestrial gravity ... it is the only power in the world that seems to overcome the so-called laws of nature." In prayer, God places in our hands a kind of omnipotence, enabling us to overcome even unchangeable natural law. Hear the affirmation of the Master, "Therefore, I say to you, *whatever* you ask for in your prayers, believe it granted and it will be granted" (Mark 11:24, *Rieu*). And if that is not enough to kindle expectation and stimulate faith, consider this: "If two of you shall agree ... as touching *anything* that they shall ask, it shall be done for them ..." (Matt. 18:19).

Strangely enough, the human heart is so beset by unbelief that these staggering and all-inclusive promises— "whatever," "anything"—instead of stimulating our faith tend to paralyze it. The mind busily sets to work to conjure up reasons why these universal words can't mean exactly what they say. But they *do* mean exactly what they say.

Unbelief has always shackled omnipotence. Faith releases its might. And faith is not credulity, it is confidence. It rests its weight on the divine guarantee of the infallible Word. It joyously believes that to the God who "calls into existence the things that do not exist," *nothing* is impossible.

Faith is the substance of things hoped for. Hebrews 11:1

"Faith is the substance of things hoped for," and not mere shadow. It is not less than sight, but more. Sight only shows the outward forms of things; faith gives the substance. You can rest on substance, feed on substance. Christ dwelling in the heart by faith is power indeed.

J. Hudson Taylor, *Great Is Thy Faithfulness*

Unceasing Prayer

Pray without ceasing. I Thessalonians 5:17

Was this exhortation to the Christians at Thessalonica merely a counsel of perfection? Did Paul really consider it an attainable ideal to "pray always with all prayer and supplications"? (Eph. 6:18)

Undoubtedly to him this was both a glorious possibility and an actual experience. "Unceasingly I make mention of you in my prayers," he wrote. "Night and day praying exceedingly." "Praying at all seasons." "Watch ye, and pray always." On God's side, Paul's experience of unceasing prayer sprang from the working of the Spirit of prayer within him. His own part was the response of a sensitive and willing spirit. Nor did he limit himself to formal seasons of prayer. Those informal, involuntary, bursts of prayer native to the praying heart were normal for him. Charles H. Spurgeon once said that for years he had not known a half-hour in which he had not consciously prayed. To him, through disciplined habit, unceasing prayer had become almost instinctive to him, as natural as breathing. To the Spirit-indwelt heart every occurrence, every occasion, becomes the inspiration of prayer.

But prayer is not an exercise of the conscious mind alone. Henry Moorhouse, the great evangelist of a past generation, frequently prayed aloud in his sleep. "I sleep, but my heart waketh" (Song of Songs 5:2), was true of him. Even in sleep, the ever-burning fire of the Holy Spirit within caused the fragrant incense of prayer to ascend from the altar of his heart.

It is our privilege to form this blessed habit, to find in God a Friend *always* within call, to use *everything* as an occasion for prayer. Through intimacy and obedience we may know the Holy Spirit's unceasing intercession *within* us (Rom. 8:27), just as on high our Great High Priest never ceases interceding *for* us (Heb. 7:25).

We give ourselves continually to prayer. Acts 6:4

Shall we not, each one of us, determine to labor more in prayer and cultivate more intimate communion with God by His help, thinking less of what we do and more of what He does? Then He will in actual deed be glorified in and through us!

J. HUDSON TAYLOR, *When You Pray*

Unanswered Prayer

Have faith in God. Mark 11:22

"It is easy to become a fatalist in regard to prayer. It is easier to see unanswered prayer as the will of God than to deliberately reason out the causes of defeat." But should we be less honest in our approach to this perplexing problem than a merchant to his adverse balance sheet? Perhaps our reluctance to analyze our failures in prayer is rooted in a mistaken concern for God's honor. God is more honored when we ruthlessly face our failure and diligently search for its cause than when we piously ignore it.

The underlying reason for *every* unanswered prayer is that in some way we have asked amiss (James 4:3). Could it be we have substituted faith in *prayer* for faith in *God*? Nowhere are we exhorted to have faith in *prayer*, but we are counselled: "Have faith in God" (Mark 11:22). Faced with this problem the disciples asked: "Why could not we ...?" "Because of your unbelief," the Master replied. An analysis of our prayers might bring about the disconcerting discovery that many are not the *prayer of faith* at all, only the *prayer of hope*, or even of despair. We earnestly hope they will answered, but have no unshakable assurance that they will. However, God has agreed to answer only the prayer of faith. "Whatever you pray for and ask, believe that you have got it, and you *shall have it*" (Mark 11:24), *Moffatt*). Don't think the translator got his tenses wrong! It is we who have got our attitude wrong!

Another prolific cause of defeat in the prayer life is a secret sympathy with sin. "If I regard"—cling to—"iniquity in my heart, the Lord will not hear me." So let us search out and correct the causes of our unanswered petitions.

Shall he not ... freely give us all things? Romans 8:32

We never have to wait for God's giving. God has already "blessed us with all spiritual blessings in heavenly places in Christ." We may reverently say, He has nothing more to give for He has given His all. Yet we may be unable to receive all He has given if the self-life is filling to some extent our hearts and lives.

J. HUDSON TAYLOR, *Great Is Thy Faithfulness*

Praying with Authority

Behold, I have given you authority ...
over all the power of the enemy. Luke 10:19, RSV

The missionary is engaged in a spiritual warfare against intangible and spiritual foes. For such a conflict only spiritual weapons are adequate, but they are "mighty through God to the pulling down of strongholds." Of these the most potent is the weapon of "all prayer" (Eph. 6:18), and it can be wielded by others on the missionary's behalf.

To His seventy eager disciples the Lord to whom "all authority in heaven and on earth" had been given (Matt. 28:18) said, *"Behold, I have given you authority ... over all the power of the enemy"* (Luke 10:19, *RSV*) With this affirmation, he linked, "I saw Satan fall like lightning from heaven." The unmistakable inference was that, through exercising their delegated authority, they too would see the overthrow of Satan in their sphere of responsibility. Nor were they disappointed. "Lord, even the demons are subject to us *through thy name*," the radiant missionaries reported.

This promised authority was not withdrawn, but when they lost vital faith in Christ's promise His disciples were powerless to deliver a demon-possessed boy (Matt. 17:19). They were paralyzed by their own unbelief. After His resurrection the Master once again affirmed their privilege. "Making use of My name"—My authority—"they shall expel demons" (Mark 16:17, *Weymouth*).

In this way, we have been given this same spiritual authority today over Satan's power, to be exercised through prayer. Christ, by His death and victorious resurrection, has "destroyed"—rendered powerless—the devil. As members of His body, united by a living faith, we may participate in His victory, not only for ourselves, but on behalf of those in distant lands. His triumph becomes ours.

As we pray, making use of Christ's authority so clearly delegated to us, we can be instrumental in binding "the strong man" in any given situation. The missionary can then "spoil his goods."

If ye have faith as a grain of mustard seed...
Matthew 17:20

Though your faith were small as a grain of mustard seed it would be enough to move mountains. We need a faith that rests on a great God, and that expects Him to keep His own word and to do just as He has promised.

J. HUDSON TAYLOR, *Great Is Thy Faithfulness*

Praying for Missionaries

... ye also helping together by prayer for us.
2 Corinthians 1:11

"Strive together with me in your prayers to God *for* me," the great missionary apostle pleaded (Rom. 15:30). In spite of his great gifts of nature and of grace, we search in vain for any sign of conscious adequacy. "Who is sufficient for these things?" Paul asks. Small wonder if his weaker successors crave the intercession of God's people. But what shall we ask God for them?

A veteran missionary facing the fierce opposition of the Adversary in the South Seas wrote: "There is nothing more profitable, more priceless, that you can ask for us than that in spite of physical weariness, frequent infirmities and the care of multiplying converts, we may be *enabled to remain on our knees.* For there is a praying in detail to be done if the infant churches are to grow and prosper." This is a key subject for intercession. Our prayers can make the prayers of our missionary friends especially potent and prevailing.

Note in these verses the juxtaposition of the hard-pressed missionary's extremity and his deliverance. "We were pressed out of measure, beyond strength ... but God delivered us ... *ye also helping together by prayer for us*" (2 Cor. 1:8-11). Our intercession may be instrumental in delivering missionaries from "unreasonable and wicked men" (2 Thess. 3:2). *Closed doors* can be made to swing open on their unwilling hinges as we lay hold of God (Col. 4:2).

Though preaching presented no difficulty to Paul, he entreated the Ephesians, "Ask on my behalf *that words may be given me*, so that, outspoken and fearless, I may make known the truths of the Good News" (Eph. 6:19, *Weymouth*).

Joshua prevailed in the conflict in the valley only while

Moses' hands were raised to heaven. When they grew slack and fell, Amalek prevailed. We can have the strategic upholding ministry of Aaron and Hur.

Workers together with Him. 2 Corinthians 6:1

I so want you to realize this principle of working with God and asking Him for everything. If the work is at the command of God, then we can go to Him in full confidence for workers; and when God gives the workers, we can go to Him for means to supply their needs.

J. HUDSON TAYLOR, *God's Fellow Workers*

Audacious Praying

Whatsoever ye shall ask the Father in My name,
He will give it to you. John 16:23

How tame and insipid is much modern praying—a respectable request for a minimum expenditure and exhibition of divine power. Seldom do our petitions rise above the level of natural thought or previous experience. Do we ever dare to pray for the unprecedented? The whole atmosphere of the age tends to make us minimize what we can expect of God. Yet His Word reveals that the extent of legitimate expectation is literally without limits.

As though to anticipate our reluctance to ask audaciously, God employs every universal term in our language in His promises to the praying soul. Here they are: Whatsoever, wheresoever, whensoever, whosoever, all, any, every. Take one such promise. "*Whatsoever* ye shall ask the Father in my name, He will give it you" (John 16:23). Trace the other words in their relation to prayer and note how they encourage large petitions. It has been said that God's only limitation and condition of prayer is found in the character of the one who prays—"According to your *faith* be it unto you."

God delights to respond to daring prayer. How quickly He responded to the audacity of the Syrophoenician woman though she had no right to claim an answer. He encourages us to ask as freely for the impossible as for the possible. To Him all difficulties are the same size—less than Himself. Because this was so Jesus said, "If ye have faith as a grain of mustard seed ye shall say unto *this mountain*, Remove hence... and it shall remove; and *nothing shall be impossible* unto you" (Matt. 17:20). In the parallel passage, it is a tree and not a mighty mountain. But audacious prayer is no more dismayed by a mountain than a tree, since "all things *are possible to him that believeth."*

He is faithful that promised. Hebrews 10:23

If any of you were offered a Bank of England note, whether for five pounds or for five thousand pounds, you would never doubt the value of it. You would take the words printed on it as sure. And are not the words printed in this Book as sure? No part of the Book is unworthy of our belief. It is either God's Word or it is not.

J. HUDSON TAYLOR, *Great Is Thy Faithfulness*

Why United Prayer?

... But prayer was made without ceasing
of the church unto God. Acts 12:5

The fact that unity gives birth to strength is a principle of grace as well as of nature. A number of Christians uniting in prayer for a given person or objective brings special power into operation. Their unison demonstrates that oneness which God delights to see and acknowledge (John 17:11). Both Scripture and contemporary experience indicate there is a cumulative power in united praying. Faith is infectious, and infection spreads where numbers congregate. Unbelief thrives more readily in isolation. A fire can be kindled with a single stick only with great difficulty.

Our Lord suggested the intensification of prayer force in united praying when he said, "If two of you agree on earth about anything they ask, it will be done for them" (Matt. 18:19, *RSV*). At a united prayer meeting the mighty power of Pentecost was unleashed (Acts 2:1, 2). When the believers "lifted up their voices together to God" the place was shaken (Acts 4:24, 31). The prayer of the whole Church secured Peter's release (Acts 12:5). The missionary enterprise had its birth in a united prayer meeting of church leaders (Acts 13:1-4).

The effective fervent prayer of a righteous man can accomplish much. But Scripture and experience combine to teach that the united prayers of many righteous accomplish still more.

These all continued with one accord in prayer and supplication.
Acts 1:14

Not many days after this, in answer to united and continued

prayer, the Holy Spirit did come upon them, and they were all filled ... Since the days before Pentecost, has the whole Church ever put aside every other work, and waited on God for ten days, that that power might be manifested? We have given too much attention to method and to machinery and to resources, and too little to the source of power.

J. Hudson Taylor, *When You Pray*

Importunate Praying

They must always pray and never lose heart.
Luke 18:1, *Phillips*

Our Lord taught His disciples by contrast as well as by comparison. Contrary to what may superficially appear to be the teaching of two parables recorded in Luke's Gospel, God is neither a cranky neighbor unwilling to get up to grant our requests (Luke 11:5), nor is He a greedy judge dispensing reluctant justice (Luke 18:7). He is illustrating one of the secrets of prevailing prayer. If an ungenerous neighbor can in the end be coerced by his friend's shameless persistence (the very word used) into granting his request, how much more will their Heavenly Father give them what they need? If an unjust judge can be badgered into giving justice to a wronged widow simply because he is wearied to death with her appeals, *how much more* will God respond to the urgent cries of His children?

Half-hearted asking comes away empty-handed. Lukewarmness in prayer, as in everything else, is revolting to God. Shameless persistence, an urgency which will not be denied, returns with the desired favor in its hands. Shameless asking brought the petitioning friend as many loaves as he needed. His first "asking" met with curt refusal. Then he began to "seek," to implore his neighbor's help in his distress, only to be denied again. At last he resorted to "knocking" and hammered at the door until insistence triumphed over obstinate refusal. The same shameless persistence secured for the widow the vindication and compensation she had so long and vainly sought.

That "they must always pray and never lose heart" was our Lord's word to the disciples. God may not always give at our first asking. He may have something important to teach us as we "call upon Him day and night." We may

for those we intercede for, or are our prayers costless and crossless?

If it die, it bringeth forth much fruit. John 12:24

Fruit-bearing involved cross-bearing. "Except a corn of wheat falls into the ground and die, it abideth alone." We know how the Lord Jesus became fruitful—not just by bearing His cross, but by dying on it. Do we know much fellowship with Him in this?

J. HUDSON TAYLOR, *Fruit Bearing*

Prayer and the Promises

Every promise of God finds its affirmative in him,
and through him can be said the final Amen,
to the glory of God.
2 Corinthians 1:20, *Phillips*

A promise by God is a pledge by God. It provides the guarantee and forms the basis of the prayer of faith. The stability of a promise rests on the character and resources of the One who makes it, in the same way the value of a check depends on the probity and resources of the one who signs it. The character and fidelity of God vouch for the credibility of the promises He makes.

It is entirely with such promises that the prayer of faith is concerned. As we claim a promise of the Word of God, the Holy Spirit imparts the faith to believe that its terms will be fulfilled in the context of our prayer. With God, promise and performance are inseparable.

But promises must be distinguished from facts. We accept a stated fact of God's Word, but we plead a promise. When God proclaims a fact, faith accepts and acts on it. When God makes a promise, we comply with its conditions, claim its fulfillment and receive the promised favor. The function of the prayer of faith is to turn God's promises into facts of experience. The patriarchs obtained the fulfillment of God's promises through faith (Heb. 11:33), and turned them into personal experience.

The prayer of faith is neither based on outward circumstances nor on inward feelings. The prayer of faith finds it greatest opportunity when sight brings no helpful vision and comfortable emotions are largely absent. It springs from the naked promise or affirmation of the Word of God. It proceeds only from a divine guarantee. The prayer of faith is the power which converts promise into performance.

The eyes of the Lord are over the righteous, and His ears are open unto their prayers. 1 Peter 3:12

From the commencement of my Christian life I was led to feel that the promises were very real, and that prayer was, in sober matter of fact, transacting business with God. This could be on one's own behalf, or on behalf of those for whom one sought His blessing.

J. Hudson Taylor, *When You Pray*

Prayer is Warfare

*The weapons of our warfare are ... mighty through God
to the pulling down of strongholds.*
2 Corinthians 10:4

Prayer is not pious daydreaming; it is spiritual warfare. "Ours is not a conflict with mere flesh and blood," Paul says. Then what is it? It is conflict "with the despotisms, the empires, the forces that govern this dark world—the spiritual hosts of evil arrayed against us in the heavenly warfare" (Eph. 6:12, *Weymouth*). But what an unequal contest! What a frightening prospect to someone conscious of his own weakness! Yet it is to such a conflict we have been committed.

What is the divine strategy? The fulcrum on which the battle turns is our ability to pray the right way. It is a spiritual as well as a military maxim that the best defense is attack. Our Commander's plan is for His Church to constantly attack on all fronts. Nowhere does he envision a Church on the defensive. It is to press the battle to the very gates of hell, and they "shall not prevail against it" (Matt. 16:18). The devil's last line of defense is unable to withstand that victorious assault.

What is our weapon? Our Leader has placed in our hands the irresistible sword of the Spirit which defeated the devil in the wilderness—the Word of God. But its aggressive and conquering power is released only through the prayer of faith. Our instructions are, "Take the sword of the Spirit ... praying always with all prayer and supplication in the Spirit ... with all perseverance" (Eph. 6:17-18). This is no mere passive praying. Only aggressive prayer based on the Word of God dislodges the enemy from his citadel. For "the weapons of our warfare are ... mighty through God to the pulling down of strongholds" (2 Cor. 10:4). Such praying releases all the resources of God and brings them into use on the field of battle. Costly? Yes, but also conquering!

Continuing instant in prayer.   Romans 12:12

Don't be disheartened if you meet with difficulties. All things are working together for good, as we shall see in due time. Pray much. Satan is a terrible reality, so is the flesh; but greater is He who is within us. If God be with us, who can overcome us?

J. HUDSON TAYLOR, *When You Pray*

Abraham—Logic in Prayer

Abraham drew near, and said, Wilt thou also destroy
the righteous with the wicked?
Genesis 18:16-33

The processes of prayer and answer are not irrational. In fact, God encourages argument in prayer. While He requires submission to His revealed will, He is not pleased with languid passivity. "'Set forth your case,' says the Lord, 'Bring forth your proofs'" (Isaiah 41:21, *RSV*). We are invited to muster and present the strongest possible arguments for our petition and to press it with logic and vigor.

Confronted with the imminent doom of Sodom, home of his nephew Lot, Abraham, one of the great praying men of the Bible, does just this. His first recourse is prayer to the God with whom he enjoyed such unique intimacy that they actually shared secrets (v. 17). In the intensity of his desire, Abraham mixes audacity with argument and petition with pleading. Observe his holy daring as he intercedes. Note his growing confidence as he organizes his appeals. "Wilt thou indeed destroy the righteous with the wicked? Far be that from thee! Shall not the Judge of all the earth do right?" (vs. 23-25). He argues that such action would compromise God's moral character and tarnish His honor. As God graciously responds, Abraham returns time and again with larger demands, tempering his boldness with suitable reverence. "I am but dust and ashes." "Let not the Lord be angry." He ceases his suit upon reaching what he undoubtedly considered the smallest possible number of righteous people in Sodom.

His optimism proved unwarranted. He stopped pleading before he exhausted the mercy and grace of God, and therefore was unable to save Sodom from its doom. Nevertheless, his intercession snatched his nephew from the very jaws of death, for "God remembered Abraham and delivered Lot."

My soul, wait thou only upon God. Psalm 62:5

To most of God's children there come times of sudden awakening when some unexpected trial, illness or bereavement reveals, with startling effect, how, all unconsciously perhaps, our souls were not waiting "only upon God," but were leaning on an instrument, or on circumstances. Surely, surely, He should not be our last resource, but the first to whom we turn in our difficulties, whether small or great.

J. HUDSON TAYLOR, *God's Guiding Hand*

Moses—Steadfastness in Prayer

His hands were steady until the going down of the sun.
Exodus 17:8-14

"Then came Amalek and fought ... and Joshua discomfited Amalek." Between these cryptic sentences stands a third. "I will stand on the top of the hill with the rod of God in my hand." Here is a pictorial presentation of God's missionary strategy—chosen men interlocked with the foe, a chosen man exercising his authority in prayer. No possible connection is apparent between these isolated men, yet their functions were inextricably linked. In the fluctuations of battle the key to final victory was in the hands, not of the fighters on the field, but of the intercessor on the mount.

Prayer is more potent than armies. It was the weaponless hand of prayer that controlled the issues of battle. "When Moses lifted up his hand, Israel prevailed: and when he let down his hand Amalek prevailed."

Holding our hands high in prayer can be exhausting work. As the tides of battle ebbed and flowed, "Moses' hands grew weary." The inactivity of praying on the mount is a much greater test of spiritual stamina than battling in the valley. When Moses could no longer stand, he sat. When he could no longer raise his hands, he summoned help. *He must not fail Joshua in the valley*. At whatever cost, the rod of God must be held aloft.

Joshua must fight as though there was no uplifted rod on the mountain. Moses must pray as if there was no drawn sword in the valley. "Which things are an allegory." Divinely chosen warriors are battling satanic powers in distant lands. The final issue lies in the hands of distant intercessors, who have been entrusted with divine authority (Luke 11:10). Only as their hands are "steady unto the going down of the sun" will Amalek be utterly destroyed.

That I may know Him. Philippians 3:10

Oh, to know Him! How good, how great, how glorious—our God and Father, our God and Savior, our God and Sanctifier: to know Him! Pray on and labor on. Don't be afraid of the toil; don't be afraid of the cross; they will pay well.

J. HUDSON TAYLOR, *When You Pray*

Daniel—Conflict in Prayer

*Fear not, Daniel ... thy words were heard ... but the prince of
the kingdom of Persia withstood me...* Daniel 10:12-14

Elijah was a brilliant meteor in Israel's firmament, whereas
Daniel was a fixed star. For over seventy years, and through
five reigns as prime minister of mighty Babylon, he wielded a prodigious influence. The divine record compresses his
secret into four words: "He kneeled ... as aforetime"—a
three times per daily spiritual exercise. The tyrant king
could not compel him to bow to his golden image. The jeal-
ous courtiers could not keep him on his feet when the
appointed hour for prayer arrived.

Ezekiel selected Daniel as one of the great intercessors of
Old Testament times (Ezek. 14:14). It was his praying which
broke the chains of the Babylonian captivity, setting Israel
free to fulfill the divine purpose. But it was no desultory and
sporadic prayer. It took seventy years of faithful intercession
before he witnessed Israel's emancipation. Nor was his praying uncontested. His visible enemies endeavored to keep him
from the act of prayer. His invisible adversaries opposed the
answering of his prayer. "The prince of the kingdom of Persia
withstood me one and twenty days" (10:13).

Daniel learned that invisible forces rule the world, that
the course of global events can be influenced by the persistent praying of one man. Once the angel Gabriel came to him
while in the act of prayer (9:21). Now it was Michael who
became his ally against his unseen foe (10:13), assuring him
that his prayer was heard from the very moment it was
uttered, though the answer was delayed for three weeks.

Prayer is often a contest between angels who minister
and demons who hinder. Prayer unanswered is not always
prayer denied. Sometimes it is prayer delayed through
invisible spiritual activity. It was Daniel's continued

wrestling on earth while the battle raged in the heavenlies, that finalized the victory.

Hold fast till I come. Revelation 2:25

I believe we shall see those successful who can abide God's time with patience. If the storm comes, let us bow to it, but hold on to our anchor. If we cannot make much headway, let us try to hold on, and in time, wind and tide will change. God may try us; He will not fail us.

J. HUDSON TAYLOR, *Great Is Thy Faithfulness*

Elijah—Faith in Prayer

... subject to like passions as we are, and he prayed earnestly
James 5:17, 1 Kings 17:21,18:36,37,42

God's man for the hour is the man who has mastered the prayer of faith. Because of his prayers, Elijah flamed like a meteor across the midnight of Israel's apostasy. Man of like passions with us, he was a man of unlike passion in prayer. He threw all the fiery forces of his nature into his praying (James 5:17). Before ever he crashed on to the stage of Israel's history, he had graduated in the school of prayer. He was no novice in the art of taking hold of God. Only long intimacy with the Almighty could give birth to such audacious prayers of faith.

Who else had the serene faith to expect God to stop the beneficent course of nature at his word (James. 5:17)? Who else had offered a prayer that rent the sky with heaven's vindicating flame (1 Kings 18:38)? His prayers had prevailed in private before he put God to the test in public. His faith created the atmosphere in which God could work His miracles. Because he stood consciously before God he could stand fearlessly before the king (18:15). The divine response to his prayer of faith demonstrated to the nation that God was God, and brought them on their faces in awe before Him (18:39).

Elijah's faith had the divine promise of rain on which to rest (18:1). But he had no promise of fire. Yet so well did he know his God that he dared to commit Him so that He could not fail to respond without compromising His own character and existence (18:36, 37). His prayers invaded a realm never before challenged—the domain of death (17:21, 22). When he prayed for rain, he did not require the comforting assurance of sight (18:43). He could believe God without any evidence to the senses. This is the prayer of faith.

evil one." God is still looking for men and women whose ambition expresses itself in a prayer like that of Jabez.

———————

The Lord thy God, the faithful God which keepeth covenant.
Deuteronomy 7:9

God has been faithful to us, as far as we have gone out on His promises and have trusted His faithfulness; but how little we have done so! How small, after all, have been our prayers and expectations, seeing we have such a God to do with.

J. HUDSON TAYLOR, *Great Is Thy Faithfulness*

Hezekiah—Simplicity in Prayer

And Hezekiah ... spread it before the Lord.
Isaiah 37:14, 38:2-5

Simplicity is not necessarily stupidity. A man may be child-like without being childish. Indeed, faith is always charac-terized by simplicity. Hezekiah, king, soldier, and poet, was artless in his relationship with God. Rabshakeh and his overwhelming hosts surrounded the royal city. He used every trick to shake the morale of the people. When con-fronted with a taunting and blasphemous letter from Rabshakeh, Hezekiah's spontaneous reaction was to com-mit the matter to his God. "Hezekiah went up unto the house of the Lord and spread it before the Lord." Behold the simplicity of faith! As though God could not read the letter when rolled up! But his was a simplicity which moved the heart and hand of God. Hear the sequel. "Then the angel of the Lord ... smote ... of the Assyrians a hundred and four score and five thousand." Mighty armies are defenseless before the feeble breath of prayer. Hezekiah's enemies were destroyed not by his military might or strat-egy but by his simple prayer.

To ask God to reconsider and revoke His decree pre-sented no insuperable problem to this man of simple heart. When Isaiah communicated to him God's edict that he would die, his faith was not staggered. As was his habit, he turned to God in prayer (38:2, 3). And in response to his prayer God changed His mind!

Think of the height to which his prayer soared. Not only did he have no promise of healing as a basis for his faith, but he had the decree of God that he should die. In spite of this he pressed his plea, and God responded magnificently. After this experience, we need never doubt the power of prayer to move the hand of God. The man who knows God may even reverently challenge His decrees.

He will fulfill the desire of them that fear Him.
Psalm 145:19

He knew the desire of my heart, and simply trusting like a child, I brought everything to Him in prayer. Thus I experienced, quite early, how He is willing to help and strengthen and to fulfill the desire of those who fear Him.

J. HUDSON TAYLOR, *When You Pray*

Hannah—Wordless Prayer

Hannah spoke in her heart.
I Samuel 1:13

Strong, spiritual leaders usually have strong praying mothers. It is not mere coincidence that Bible history frequently records the ancestry of its great men. Praying Samuels come from praying Hannahs. Indeed, Samuel was the direct creation of his mother's wordless praying. "The Lord remembered her; and in due time Hannah ... bore a son, and she called his name Samuel, for ... I have asked him of the Lord" (1:19, 20, *RSV*).

The traditional shame of her childlessness was crushing her spirit. Her rival, Elkanah's other wife, "used to provoke her sorely, to irritate her" (1:6, *RSV*). Tried beyond endurance, she repaired to the temple and there poured out her soul to a listening God. The aging priest, Eli, dozing on his seat "observed her mouth. Hannah was speaking in her heart; only her lips moved, and her voice was not heard" (1:13). Eli mistook her inarticulate grief for maudlin intoxication. "How long will you be drunken?" he chided her. She protested that her trouble was grief of heart. She was beside herself with the intensity of her supplication, a prototype of those for whom "the Spirit himself intercedes with sighs too deep for words" (Rom. 8:26, *RSV*). Some prayers affect us too deeply for formal speech.

Hannah accompanied her prayer with a vow. "If thou wilt ... remember ... I will give" (1:11). She kept her promise, and as soon as Samuel was weaned, she presented him to the Lord for life. "And they worshiped the Lord there" (1:28). But now it is not wordless praying. Fervent, passionate words flow out of her heart in an uncontrollable tide of adoration (2:1-10). It was a rhapsody worthy of those of Miriam and Deborah and Mary. Small wonder that Samuel's early years, spent in the company of his praying mother, made him a man with a ministry bathed in prayer.

Ask what I shall give thee. 1 Kings 3:5

Now let's stop and ask ourselves; what do we desire? And then let us claim the promise at once. Have we loved ones unsaved? Have we difficulties to conquer? Have we mountains to remove? Then let us take it to the Lord in prayer.

J. HUDSON TAYLOR, *When You Pray*

Nehemiah—Spontaneous Prayer

For what dost thou make request? So I prayed ...
Nehemiah 2:4

True patriot that he was, Nehemiah's heart was deeply distressed at the desolation of his beloved Zion. Like all other spiritual men he turned his heart burden into prayer. "I wept, and mourned, and fasted, and prayed" (1:4). And what a model prayer it was, combining adoration, confession, argument and petition (1:5-11). The sheer impossibility of his desire being granted—leave of absence from the side of a despotic Eastern tyrant for four months—did not daunt his faith. He was sure of his God.

God can never resist faith. As Nehemiah prayed, God worked in the king's heart and suddenly the prayed-for opportunity came (2:1-6). Between the despot's unexpected question and Nehemiah's daring request, he found time for bursts of spontaneous prayer. "So I prayed to the God of heaven" (2:4). Not only was he granted leave to go to Jerusalem, but he received full provision for the expedition as well. Once again prayer had invaded the realm of the impossible.

His plan of campaign for the restoration of the city wall was simple. "So I prayed ... so built we the wall." He prayed as he worked and worked as he prayed. Did enemies mock and hinder? He utters a spontaneous prayer and keeps on building (4:4-6). Did they threaten attack? "We made our prayer ... and set a watch" (4:9). Prayer was no substitute for earnest effort and careful preparation, and work was no hindrance to prayer. He did not reserve his prayers for special occasions, they pervaded all his activities. He worked no mighty miracle. He saw no spectacular vision. But the prayer of his burdened, believing heart secured dramatic results. In fifty-two short days he was

being "thoroughly convinced in all that concerns the will of God."

It was Epaphras' kneeling which kept the Colossians standing.

There shall be with thee, for all manner of workmanship, every willing man. **1 Chronicles 28:21**

How are we to get the beautiful combination of willing, skillful men for the work of God? They are promised to our loyal Master. They must be sought from Him. They must be claimed by faith and prayer, as Christ Himself directed His disciples to pray to the Lord of the harvest to thrust forth laborers into His own harvest.

J. HUDSON TAYLOR, *God's Fellow Workers*

Prayer Takes Time

Are there not twelve hours in the day?
John 11:9

Which of us has not experienced the difficulty of insufficient time for prayer? At least we tend to excuse ourselves by saying we do not have sufficient time. The late Dr. J. H. Jowett was not sympathetic to such an excuse. "I think one of the common phrases of our day," he wrote, "is the one by which we express our permanent lack of time. We repeat it so often that by the very repetition we have deceived ourselves into believing it. It is never the supremely busy men who have no time. So compact and systematic is the regulation of their day that, whenever you make a demand on them, they seem able to find additional corners to offer for unselfish service. I confess, as a minister, that the men to whom I most hopefully look for additional service are the busiest men."

Let us face the fact squarely and without excuse—*Each of us has as much time as anyone else in the world.* As in the parable of the pounds, we have each been entrusted with the same amount of time, but not all use it in such a way that we produce a tenfold return. True, we do not all have the same capacity, but that fact is recognized in the parable, and the reward for the servant with the smaller capacity but equal faithfulness is the same. We are not responsible for our capacity. We are responsible for the strategic investment of our time. If we consider prayer as a high priority, we will so arrange our day to make time for it. When we have comparatively little to carry in our case it seems as full as when we have a lot, because the less we have the more carelessly we pack it. The man who claims to have no time is most likely guilty of "careless packing."

What practical steps can be taken to safeguard the

securing of sufficient time for prayer?

Stop Leaks. Do not consider your day only in terms of hours, but in smaller areas of time. If we look after the minutes, the hours will look after themselves. Few men packed more into a lifetime than Dr. F. B. Meyer. Of him it was said that like John Wesley he divided his life into spaces of five minutes, and tried to make each one count for God. You would expect this to create intolerable strain. But not with Dr. Meyer. According to his biographer, "his calm manner was not the sleep of an inactive mind, it was more like the sleep of a spinning top." Just a little while before his departure he said to a friend, "I think I am an example of what the Lord can do with a man who concentrates on doing one thing at one time." The secret of Charles Darwin's achievements, it is said, was that he knew the difference between ten minutes and a quarter of an hour.

D. E. Hoste, successor to Hudson Taylor, in a life acknowledged to be extremely full, always made time for a deep and full prayer life. He gave prayer priority in his life because he considered it most important. But he did not arrive immediately at the mastery of his time. "It is easy to waste time," he wrote.

"The missionary after breakfast may sit down to read the newspaper, or let time slip by in another way. But this cannot be done in business life. I have found the need of much watchfulness and self-discipline in this matter during my years in the interior. A sensitive conscience about the use of time needs to be maintained."

Study Priorities. Much time which is not actually wasted, is spent on things of only secondary importance. A fool has been described as a man who has missed the proportion of things. Some of us have the unfortunate habit of being so engrossed in the secondary that we have no time left for the primary. We give such undue attention to petty details that matters of major importance are squeezed out. This is especially the case where prayer is concerned, and our adversary will do all in his power to aid and abet. Check to see whether the essentially spiritual is receiving adequate time, or whether the best is being relegated to a secondary place by that which is good.

Our Lord indicated that the secret of successful living was to sacrifice the pearl of inferior value for the pearl of surpassing worth. Are you doing the most important things, or do you procrastinate, substituting the secondary which makes less stringent demands on you? Weigh carefully the respective values of the opportunities and responsibilities which claim your attention. Omit altogether, or give a very minor place to things of little importance. John Wesley used to say, "Never be unemployed, and never be triflingly employed."

The Impelling Motive. To effect a radical change in our use of time so as to make more time for prayer will require strength of purpose and a deep dependence on the Lord's enabling. Not all of us naturally possess inflexible wills. But our wills can be reinforced. We can and should be "strengthened with might through His Spirit in the inner man."

The use of time depends largely on the pressure of motive. Are there motives compelling enough to enable us to change the pattern of our lives, to counter long-indulged habits of laxity in the use of time? Henry Martyn found it impossible to waste an hour in his translation work because of the vision he had of nations waiting for the truth locked up in the book he was translating. The need of a lost world proved an impelling motive to redeem the hours. The driving force in the life of our Lord was revealed in one of His incidental sayings, "I do always those things that please Him." And for Him there were always 24 hours in the day. There might not always be time to eat, but always He made time to pray. There will always be time for everything that is within the will of God.

Search me, O God, and know my heart. Psalm 139:23

Let us ask Him to search us and remove all that hinders His work in us in larger measures. If our Bibles or secret prayer have been neglected, let us confess the evil before God and claim His promised forgiveness, carefully avoiding such occasions of weakness for the future.

J. HUDSON TAYLOR, *When You Pray*

THE PRAYER OF FAITH

J O Fraser

Prayer Determination

The first missionary to the Lisu people of the Upper Salween was going through a deep testing. It was not the privation, nor the loneliness of this isolated outpost, nor the rigors of scaling the steep mountain walls to find tribal settlements, nor even the difficulty of making himself at home with these utterly primitive folk—no, none of these things troubled him. But the lack of abiding fruit in the hearts of the Lisu people—this was his constant burden. "Give me Lisu converts," he cried from the heart, "and I can truly say I will be happy even in a pigsty."

From Fraser's journal:

JANUARY 1, 1916. Must watch against getting up too late these intensely cold mornings. The indwelling Christ is my successful weapon against all sin these days—praise Him!

Sunday, Jan. 2. An earnest desire to save souls is on me, but prayer is rather unstable. I must regain my equilibrium in the prayer life. I must maintain, also, my abiding in Christ by prayer without ceasing (silent), which I am now finding blessedly possible. Romans 6 is not now my weapon so much as John 15.

Tuesday, Jan. 4. Finished Finney's autobiography; much help received from it. Finney's strong point is the using of *means* to an *end*. My own leading is ... along that line also. I do not intend to be one of those who bemoan little results while "resting in the faithfulness of God." My cue is to take hold of the faithfulness of God and use the means necessary to secure big results.

Sunday, Jan. 16. Not a single person at service in the morning .... The walls of Jericho fell down "by *faith*." Of all the instances of faith in Hebrews 11, this corresponds most nearly to my case. But not faith only was necessary; the wall fell down after it had been compassed about for seven days. Seven days' *patience* was required, and diligent compassing of the city every day—which seems to typify encompassing the situation by regular, systematic prayer. Here then we see God's way of success in our work, whatever it may be—a trinity of *prayer, faith* and *patience.*

Jan. 18. Prayer, today, rather on general than particular lines; patience the chief thought. Abraham was called out by God and went in blind faith. When he got to the land of promise, he found nothing but a famine—much like me with the Lisu these two years. But Abraham, or his seed, later on possessed the milk and honey of the whole land. God's time had come for Abraham but not for the Amorites. God's time has come for me, but not perhaps, just this month or this year, for the Lisu.

Am impressed, too, that I do not yet know the channels which the grace of God is going to cut out among the people here. Hence general prayer has its place, until God's plan is revealed a little more fully.

There had been a few souls who had professed Christ, but in temptation had fallen back into the ways of their old life. Fraser was brought more and more to a keen realization of the forces arrayed against him, and also of his need for believers in the homeland who would cooperate with him in prayer.

Feb. 4. No meal till 2 p.m. Thoroughly depressed about state of work at Tantsah. Feel much inclined to "let Ephraim alone," but I am torn between two alternatives, for I seem to have no leading to leave Tantsah. My prayer is not so much, "Lord lead me somewhere else," as "Lord, give me a solid church here at Tantsah."

Feb. 5. I am not taking the black, despondent view I took yesterday. The opposition will not be overcome by reasoning or by pleading, but (chiefly) by steady, persistent prayer. The *men* need not be dealt with (it is a heartbreaking job, trying to deal with a Lisu possessed by a spirit of fear) but the *powers of darkness* need to be fought. I am now setting my face like a flint: if the work seems to fail, then pray; if services, etc., fall flat, then *pray still more;*

if months slip by with little or no result, then *pray still more and get others to help you.*

Mar. 13. Cloud seems to have lifted considerably—perhaps because prayer burden fought right through .... After much pressure, even agony, in prayer for Lisu souls, enabled to break through into liberty, and to pray the definite prayer of faith for signal blessing among the Lisu during the next few months .... Real, prevailing prayer, for the first time for a week or more, and well worth the travail that led up to it .... Much peace and rest of soul after making that definite prayer, and almost ecstatic joy to think of the Lisu Christian families I am going to get.

Aug. 27. The Cross is going to hurt—let it hurt! I am going to work hard and pray hard too, by God's grace.

———————

He that abideth in Me ... bringeth forth much fruit. John 15:5

It is unbelief that saps our strength and makes everything look dark; and yet He reigns, and we are one with Him, and He is making everything happen for the very best. So we ought to always rejoice in Him, and rest, though it is not always easy. We must triumph with God, and then we shall succeed with men, and be made blessings to them.

J. HUDSON TAYLOR, *Fruit Bearing*

Prayer Cooperation

Can it be that the responsibility for a great work for God involving thousands of souls rests upon our prayer life—half a world away?

WORK ON OUR KNEES. I am feeling more and more that it is, after all, just the prayers of God's people that call down blessing on the work, whether they are directly engaged in it or not. Paul may plant and Apollos water, but it is God who gives the increase; and this increase can be brought down from heaven by believing prayer, whether offered in China or in England. We are, as it were, God's agents— used by Him to do His work, not ours. We do our part, and then can only look to Him, with others, for His blessing. If this is so, then Christians at home can do as much for foreign missions as those actually on the field. I believe it will only be known on the Last Day how much has been accomplished in missionary work by the prayers of earnest believers at home. And this, surely, is the heart of the problem. Such work does not consist in curio exhibitions, lantern lectures, interesting reports, and so on. Good as they may be, these are only the fringe, not the root of the matter. Solid, lasting missionary work is done on our knees. What I covet more than anything else, is earnest, believing prayer, and I write to ask you to continue in prayer for me and the work here.

. . . .

WHEN THE TIDE COMES IN. I cannot insist too strongly on my own helplessness among these people apart from the grace of God. Although I have been now ten years in China and have had considerable experience with both Chinese and Lisu, I find myself able to do little or nothing apart from God's going before me and working among men. Without this I feel like a man who has his boat grounded in shallow water. Pull or push as he may, he will not be able to make his boat move more than a few inches. But let the tide come in and lift his boat off the bottom—*then* he will be able to move it as far as he pleases, quite easily and without friction. It is indeed necessary for me to go around among our Lisu, preaching, teaching, exhorting, rebuking, but the amount of progress made thereby depends almost entirely on the state of the Spiritual Tide in the village—a condition which you can control upon your knees as well as I can.

. . . .

A VOLUME OF FAITH. Praying without faith is like trying to cut with a blunt knife—much labor expended to little purpose. For the work accomplished by labor in prayer depends on our faith: "According to your faith be it unto you."

I have been impressed lately with the thought that people fail in praying the prayer of faith because they do not believe that God *has* already answered, but only that He *will* some time or other answer their petitions. This is not the faith that makes prayer effective. True faith glories in the present tense, and does not trouble itself about the future. God's promises are in the present tense and are quite secure enough to set our hearts at rest. Their full outworking is often in the future, but God's word is as good as His bond and we need have no anxiety. Sometimes He gives at once what we ask, but more often He just gives His promise (Mark 11:24). Perhaps He is more glorified in this latter case, for it means that our faith is tried and strengthened. I do earnestly covet a volume of prayer for my Lisu work—but oh! for a *volume of faith* too. Will you give this?

All things are possible to him that believeth. **Mark 9:23**

People say, "Lord, increase our faith." Did not the Lord rebuke His disciples for that prayer? He said, "You do not

want a great faith, but faith in a great God. If your faith were as small as a grain of mustard seed, it would suffice to remove this mountain!"

J. Hudson Taylor, *Great Is Thy Faithfulness*

Prayer Solidarity

"I am an engineer and believe in things working. I want to see them work," Fraser used to say. And because he believed that prayer works—"If ye shall ask ... I will do" (John 14:14)—and that God means it when He guarantees results from energy spent in prayer (James 5:16-18), Fraser determined to provide prayer material for more prayer supporters so that the volume of prayer rising for the Lisu work would constantly increase.

I KNOW you will never fail me in the matter of intercession *he wrote to his mother,* but will you think and pray about getting a group of like-minded friends, whether few or many, whether in one place or scattered, to join in the same petitions? If you could form a small prayer circle I would write regularly to the members.

· · · ·

What a number of earnest, spiritually-minded Christians there are at home *Fraser wrote on his return to Tengyueh after an arduous survey trip* and how correspondingly rich are the prayer forces of the church! How I long for some of this wealth for myself and the Lisu here. I have had it in measure already, but I should very, very much like a wider circle of intercessors.

Our work among the Lisu is not going to be a bed of roses, spiritually. I know enough about Satan to realize that he will have all his weapons ready for determined opposition. He would be a missionary simpleton who expected plain sailing in *any* work of God. I will not, by God's grace, let anything deter me from going straight ahead in the path to which He leads, but I shall feel greatly strengthened if I know of a definite company of pray-ers holding me up. I am confident that the Lord is going to do a work, sooner or later, among the Lisu here.

· · · ·

About three years later: Knowing as I do the conditions of the work, its magnitude (potentially), its difficulties and the opposition it meets with, I have definitely resolved, with God's help, to enlarge the place of my tent, to lengthen my prayer cords and strengthen my intercessory stakes, to make a forward movement with regard to the Prayer Circle.

I am persuaded that the homeland is rich in godly, quiet, praying people, in every denomination. They may not be a great multitude as far as numbers are concerned, but they are "rich in faith," even if many of them be poor and of humble station. It is the prayers of such that I covet more than gold of Ophir—those good men and women who know what it is to have power with God and prevail. Will you help me, prayerfully and judiciously, to get some of these to join the circle? The work for which I am asking prayer is preaching and teaching the Word of God, pure and simple. I have no confidence in anything but the gospel of Calvary to uplift these needy people.

. . . .

After the work had begun to show the shape of things to come: The Lisu and Kachin converts would be easily able to support their own pastors, teachers and evangelists by well-advised cultivation of their own ample hillsides, and it is fitting that the mountains should bring forth supplies for the needs of those whose feet are beautiful upon them. But spiritually they are babes, and as dependent upon us as a child upon his mother. They are dependent on us out here for instruction, guidance, organization; but they are dependent on the home churches in England and America in a deeper sense, for spiritual life and power. I really believe that if every particle of prayer put up by the home churches on behalf of the infant churches of the mission field were removed, the latter would be swamped by an incoming flood of the powers of darkness. This seems actually to have happened in church history—churches losing all their power and life, becoming a mere empty name, or else flickering out altogether. Just as a plant may die for lack of watering, so may a genuine work of God die and rot for lack of prayer.

One might compare heathenism with a great mountain threatening to crush the infant church, or a great pool of stagnant water always threatening to quench the flames of Holy Ghost life and power in the native churches, and only kept dammed up by the power of God. God is able to do this and much more, but He will not do it if all of us out here and you at home sit in our easy chairs with arms folded. Why prayer is so indispensable we cannot say, but we had better recognize the fact even if we cannot explain it. Do you believe that the church of God would be alive today were it not for the high priestly intercession of the Lord Jesus Christ on the Throne? I do not: I believe it would have been dead and buried long ago. Viewing the Bible as a record of God's work on this earth, I believe that it gives a clear, ringing message to His people—from Genesis to Revelation—you must do your part.

The church of Protestant countries is well able to nourish the infant church of the Orient by a steady and powerful volume of intercessory prayer. Applying this to the work among the Tengyueh tribespeople, I feel I can say that you, and those God will yet call to join you in this prayer work, are well able to sustain the spiritual life of the Lisu and Kachin converts, as well as to increase their number many fold. It may be He has been preparing you for the unseen and spiritual parenthood of these infant Lisu converts here, however many thousand miles separate you from them.

I am not asking you just to give "help" in prayer as a sort of sideline, but I am trying to roll the main responsibility of this prayer warfare on you. I want you to take the burden of these people upon your shoulders. I want you to wrestle with God for them. I do not want so much to be a regimental commander in this matter as an intelligence officer. I shall feel more and more that a big responsibility rests upon me to keep you well informed. The Lord Jesus looks down from heaven and sees these poor, degraded, neglected tribespeople. "The travail of His soul" was for them, too. He has waited long. Will you not do your part to bring in the day when He shall "be satisfied"?

Anything must be done rather than let this prayer-service be dropped or even allowed to stagnate. We often speak of intercessory work as being of vital importance. I want to prove that I believe this in actual fact by giving my first and best energies to it, as God may lead. I feel like a business-man who perceives that a certain line of goods pays better than any other in his store, and who purposes making it his chief investment; who, in fact sees an inexhaustible supply and an almost unlimited demand for a profitable article and intends to go in for it more than for anything else. The "demand" is the lost state of these tens of thousands of Lisu and Kachin—their ignorance, their superstition, their sinfulness; their bodies, their minds, their souls; the "sup-ply" is the grace of God to meet this need—to be brought down to them by the persevering prayers of a considerable company of God's people. All I want to do is, as a kind of middleman, to bring the supply and the demand together.

Whatever ye shall ask in prayer, believing ye shall receive.
Matthew 21:22

Seeing that in days of old faith wrought such mighty wonders ... and that we have the same God ... shall we not ask great things? Believing prayer will lead to whole-hearted action, and the Lord for our encouragement says, "If two of you shall agree on earth as touching anything that they shall ask, it shall be done for them of My Father which is in heaven."

J. HUDSON TAYLOR, *When You Pray*

Prayer Procedure

*It was his own daily contact with the "darkness that can be felt"
in the battle for souls that led Fraser to share with his prayer con-
stituency some thoughts on the heart attitude which leads to effective prayer.*

PREPARE FOR PRAYER. "If two of you shall agree"—I felt,
even when praying alone, that there are two concerned in
the prayer, God and myself .... I do not think that a petition
which misses the mind of God will ever be answered (1
John 5:14). Personally, I feel the need of trusting Him to
lead me in prayer as well as in other matters. I find it helpful to preface prayer not only by meditation but by the definite request that I be directed into the channels of prayer
to which the Holy Spirit is beckoning me. I also find it helpful to make a short list, like notes prepared for a sermon,
before every season of prayer. The mind needs to be guid-
ed as well as the spirit attuned. I can thus get my thoughts
in order, and having prepared my prayer can put the notes
on the table or chair before me, kneel down and get to business.

. . . .

WITH THE UNDERSTANDING ALSO. Always remember, "I will
pray with the spirit, and I will pray with the understanding
also" (1 Cor. 14:15). Let the spirit and the understanding
work in about equal proportions. First, think over the
needs taking into account any consciousness of spirit-bur-
den. Pray, tentatively, along that line, asking God continually to *focus* your prayers. If, after covering such ground in
prayer, no "grip" comes anywhere, it is probably best to
close down at once. Do not be in a hurry to do this, but
don't press on in the energy of the flesh.

. . . .

HANNAH'S PRAYER. I was very severely disappointed about

the attitude of the Lisu of that district [near Tantsah] to the gospel. They received the Word with joy at first, as they so often do. Several announced that they were going to turn Christian, and one old man and his son seemed specially earnest. Then the spirit of fear seemed to possess them, and one by one they dropped off until no one would take a stand at all. We had to leave them as heathen as I first found them. It was a very painful experience and seemed almost to stun me for a while.

How much of our prayer is of the quality we find in Hannah's "bitterness of soul" when she "prayed unto the Lord"? How many times have we "wept sore" before the Lord? We have prayed much, perhaps, but our longings have not been deep compared with hers. We may have spent much time on our knees without our hearts going out in an agony of desire. But real supplication is the child of heartfelt desire. It cannot prevail without it. This is not an earthly desire, nor does it issue from our own sinful hearts, but it is wrought into us by God Himself. Oh, for such desires! Oh, for Hannah's earnestness, not in myself only but in all who are joining me in prayer for these poor heathen aborigines!

And is there not sufficient reason for such earnestness? We have our Peninnahs as surely as Hannah had and as God's saints have had all down the ages. David's eyes ran with rivers of water because the ungodly did not observe God's law (Ps. 119:136). Jeremiah wept with bitter lamentation because of the destruction of the holy city. Nehemiah fasted, mourned, and wept when he heard of the fresh calamities which had befallen Jerusalem. Our Lord wept before it because of its hardness of heart. The Apostle Paul had "great sorrow and unceasing pain" in his heart on account of his brethren according to the flesh (Romans 9:2).

Yes, and *we* have our "sore provocations," or should have. How else ought we to feel when we see all the ungodliness and unbelief around us on every hand? Would a light-hearted apathy become us under such circumstances?

No, indeed! And I want you, please, to join me—or, rather, share with me—in the "provocation" which is daily with me in my work among the Lisu. Let the terrible power of evil spirits among them be a provocation to *you*. Let their sinfulness, their fears, their pitiful weakness and instability be a provocation to *you*. Ask God to lay the burden upon you, and that heavily—that it may press you down upon your knees. My prayer for you is that God will work such sorrow within you that you will have no alternative but to pray. I want you to be "sore provoked" as I am.

Such a state of mind and heart is only useful, however, as it is turned into prayer. Desire, however deep, does nothing in itself any more than steam pressure in a boiler is of use unless it is allowed to drive machinery. There is a spiritual law here. A strong spiritual desire does harm rather than good if it is neglected. An earnest desire in spiritual things is a bell ringing for prayer. Not that we should wait for such desires. We should pray at all seasons, whether we are prayer-hungry or not. If we have a healthy prayer-appetite, so much the better. But if this appetite is unnoticed or unappeased, a dullness will come over us and we shall be weakened in spirit, just as lack of sufficient food weakens us in body. See, in 1 Samuel 1:15, the way in which Hannah dealt with her God-given desire. Her soul was bitter, and she "poured it out" before the Lord. Blessed bitterness!—but it must be poured out.

Ask of God ... and it shall be given. **James 1:5**

We must all get nearer to God; we must all abide in Christ; our lives must be more up to our principles and privileges, and all will be well. Let us trust for all, and we shall find all. God can bless; let us ask it in faith, and expect it. Nothing else, nothing less can satisfy Him; nothing less must satisfy us.

J. HUDSON TAYLOR, *When You Pray*

The Prayer of Faith - I

THE Scriptures speak of several kinds of prayer. There is intercession and there is supplication, there is labor in prayer and there is the prayer of faith; all perhaps the same fundamentally, but they present various aspects of this great and wonderful theme. It would not be unprofitable to study the differences between these various scriptural terms.

There is a distinction between *general* prayer and *definite* prayer. By definite prayer I mean prayer after the pattern of Matthew 21:21, 22 and John 15:7, where a definite petition is offered up and definite faith exercised for its fulfillment. Now faith must be in exercise in the other kinds of prayer also, when we pray for many and varied things without knowing the will of God in every case.

In *general prayer* I am limited by my ignorance. But this kind of prayer is the duty of us all (1 Tim. 2:1, 2), however vague it has to be. I may know very little, in detail, about the object of my prayer, but I can at any rate commend it to God and leave it with Him. It is good and right to pray, vaguely, for all people, all lands, all things, at all times.

But *definite prayer* is a very different matter. It is in a special sense "the prayer of faith." A definite request is made in definite faith for a definite answer.

Take the case of a Canadian immigrant as an illustration of the prayer of faith. Allured by the prospect of "golden grain" he leaves home for the Canadian West. He has a definite object in view. He knows very well what he is going for, and that is wheat. He thinks of the good crops he will reap and of the money they will bring him—much like the child of God who sets out to pray the prayer of faith and who has his definite object too. It may be the conversion of a son or daughter; it may be power in Christian service; it may be guidance in a perplexing situation, or a hundred and one other things—but it is *definite*. Consider the points of resemblance between the cases of the prospective

Canadian farmer and the believing Christian.

1. THE BREADTH OF THE TERRITORY. Think of the unlimited scope for the farmer in Canada. There are literally millions of acres waiting to be cultivated. No need, there, to tread on other people's toes! Room for all—vast tracts of unoccupied land just going to waste, and good land too. And so it is with us, surely. There is a vast, vast field for us to go up and claim in faith. There is enough sin, enough sorrow, enough of the blighting influence of Satan in the world to absorb all our prayer of faith, and a hundred times as many more. "There remaineth yet very much land to be possessed."

2. GOVERNMENT ENCOURAGES IMMIGRATION. Think also of the efforts the Canadian Government is making to encourage immigration. All the unoccupied land belongs to it, but settlers are so badly needed that they are offered every inducement—immigration offices established, sea passages and railway fares reduced, and grants of land made free! God is no less urgently inviting His people to pray the prayer of faith: "*Ask—ask—ask*," He is continually saying to us. He offers His inducement too: "Ask and ye shall receive, that your joy may be full." All the unoccupied territory of faith belongs to Him. And He bids us to come and occupy freely. "How long are ye slack to go in to possess the land?"

Let him ask in faith, nothing wavering. **James 1:6**

A full knowledge of the Word will often bring to our recollection appropriate promises, and thus enable us to pray with that faith and confidence which are so closely connected with answers to prayer.

J. HUDSON TAYLOR, *When You Pray*

The Prayer of Faith - II

3. FIXED LIMITS. Yet this aspect of the truth must not be over-emphasized. Though it is a blessed fact that the land is so broad, it can easily be magnified out of due proportion. The important thing is, not the vastness of the territory, but how much of it is actually assigned to us. The Canadian Government will make a grant of 160 acres to the farmer-immigrant, and no more. Why no more? Because they know very well he cannot work any more. If they were to give him 160 square miles instead of 160 acres he would not know what to do with it all. So they wisely limit him to an amount of land equal to his resources.

And it is much the same with us when praying the prayer of definite faith. The very word "definite" means "with fixed limits." We are often exhorted, and with reason, to ask great things of God. Yet there is a balance in all things, and we may go too far in this direction. It is possible "to bite off," even in prayer, "more than we can chew." There is a principle underlying 2 Corinthians 10:13* which may apply to this very matter. Faith is like muscle which grows stronger and stronger with use, rather than rubber which weakens when it is stretched. Overstrained faith is not pure faith; there is a mixture of the carnal element in it. There is no strain in the "rest of faith." It asks for definite blessings as God may lead. It does not hold back through carnal timidity nor press ahead too far through carnal eagerness.

I have definitely asked the Lord for several hundred families of Lisu believers. There are upwards of two thousand Lisu families in the Tantsah district. It might be said, "Why do you not ask for a thousand?" I answer quite frankly, "Because I have not faith for a thousand." I believe the Lord has given me faith for more than one hundred families, but not for a thousand. So I accept the limits the

* *"According to the measure of the province [limit] which God has appointed to use as a measure." (ASV)*

Lord has, I believe, given me. Perhaps God will give me a thousand; perhaps He will lead me to commit myself to this definite prayer of faith later on. This is in accordance with Ephesians 3:20, "above all we ask or think." But we must not overload faith; we must be sane and practical. Let us not claim too little in faith, but let us not claim too much either. Remember the Canadian immigrant's 160 acres. Consider, too, how the Dominion Government exercises authority in the matter of location. The Government has a say as to the *where* as well as the *how much* of the immigrant's claim. He may not wander all over the prairie at his own sweet will and elect to settle down in any place he chooses. Even in regard to the position of his farm he must consult the Government.

Do we always do this in our prayers and claims? Do we consult the Heavenly Government at the outset, or do we pray the first thing that comes to mind? Do we spend time waiting upon God to know His will before attempting to embark on His promises? That this is a principle upon which God works He has informed us very plainly in 1 John 5:14, 15. ("And this is the confidence that we have in Him, that, if we ask anything according to His will, He hears us: and if we know that He hears us, whatsoever we ask, we know that we have the petitions that we desired of Him.")

I cannot but feel that this is one cause for many unanswered prayers. James 4:3 ("Ye ask, and receive not because ye ask amiss, that ye may consume it upon your lusts.") has a broad application, and we need to search our hearts in its light. Unanswered prayers have taught me to seek the Lord's will instead of my own. I suppose we have most of us had such experiences. We have prayed and prayed and prayed, and no answer has come. The heavens above us have been as brass. Yea, blessed brass, if it has taught us to sink a little more of this ever-present self of ours into the Cross of Christ. Sometimes our petition has been such a good one, to all appearances, but that does not ensure its being of God. Many "good desires" proceed from our uncrucified selves. Scripture and experience certainly agree that those who live nearest to God are the most likely to know His will. We are called to be "filled with the knowledge of His will" (Col. 1:9). We need to know more of the fellowship of Christ's death. We need to feed on the Word of God more than we do. We need more holiness, more prayer. We shall not, then, be in such danger of mistaking His will.

It does not follow that because a thing is the will of God, He will necessarily lead *you* to pray for it. He may have other burdens for you. We must *get our prayers from God*, and pray to know His will. It may take time. God was dealing with Hudson Taylor for fifteen years before He laid upon him the burden of definite prayer for the foundation of the China Inland Mission. God is not in a hurry. He cannot do things with us until we are trained and ready for them. We may be certain He has further service, further burdens of faith and prayer to give us when we are ready for them.

He shall choose our inheritance for us. Psalm 47:4

Having carefully laid our plans and determined to carry them through, we may ask God to help us, and to prosper us in connection with them. Yet another way of working is to begin with God; to ask His plans, and to offer ourselves to Him to carry out His purposes. Going about it in this way, we ... have no responsibility save to follow as we are led.

J. HUDSON TAYLOR, *God's Guiding Hand*

The Prayer of Faith - III

4. THE CLAIM ENDORSED. Turn to the immigrant again. He has come to an agreement with the Canadian Government. He falls in with their terms, he accepts their conditions, he agrees to take over the land allotted to him. So he presents his claim at the proper quarter, and it is at once endorsed. Could anything be simpler? Nor need our claim in the presence of God be any less simple. When we once have the deep, calm assurance of His will in the matter, we put in our claim, just as a child before his father. A simple request and nothing more. No cringing, no beseeching, no tears, no wrestling. No second asking either.

In my case I prayed continually for the Tengyueh Lisu for over four years, asking many times that several hundreds of families might be turned to God. This was only general prayer, however. God was dealing with me in the meantime. You know how a child is sometimes rebuked by his parents for asking something in a wrong way—perhaps in the case of a child, for asking rudely. The parent will say, "Ask me properly." That is just what God seemed to be saying to me then: "Ask Me properly. You have been asking Me to do this for the last four years without ever really believing that I would do it—now ask *in faith*.

I felt the burden *clearly*. I went to my room alone one afternoon and knelt in prayer. I knew that the time had come for the prayer of faith. And then, fully knowing what I was doing and what it might cost me, I definitely committed myself to this petition *in faith*. I cast my burden upon the Lord and rose from my knees with the deep, restful conviction that I had already received the answer. The transaction was done. And since then (nearly a year ago now) I have never had anything but peace and joy (when in touch with God) in holding to the ground already claimed and taken. I have never repeated the request and never will: there is no need. The asking, the taking, and the receiving occupy but a few moments (Mark 11:24). It is a solemn thing to enter into a faith covenant with God. It is binding on both parties. You lift up your hand to God, you definitely ask for and receive His proffered gift—then do not go back on your faith, even if you live to be a hundred.

———————

The righteous ... are in the hand of God. Ecclesiastes 9:1

"Let us leave all in the hands of God" ... make it a matter of prayer and then leave it in the hands of God our Father. I have prayed about it, and I am sure I can trust God. He will do all things well. God knows what is best and we must learn to welcome His will, which is good, acceptable and perfect.

J. HUDSON TAYLOR, *When You Pray*

The Prayer of Faith - IV

5. GET TO WORK. To return once more to the Canadian farmer. He has put in his claim, the land has been granted, the deed made out and sealed with the official seal. Is that the end then? No! only the beginning!

He has not attained his object yet. His object is a harvest of wheat, not a patch of waste land; and there is a vast difference between the two. The Government never promised him sacks of flour all ready for export—only the land which could be made to yield them. Now is the time for him to roll up his sleeves and get to work. He must build his homestead, get his livestock, call in laborers, clear the ground, plow it and sow his seed. The Government says to him in effect, "We have granted your claim—now go and work it."

And this distinction is no less clear in the spiritual realm. God gives us the ground in answer to the prayer of faith, but not the harvest. That must be worked for in co-operation with Him. Faith must be followed up by works, prayer-works. Salvation is of grace, but it must be worked out if it is to become ours (Phil. 2:12) . And the prayer of faith is just the same. It is given to us by free grace, but it will never be ours till we follow it up, work it out. Faith and works must never be divorced, for indolence will reap no harvest in the spiritual world. I think the principle will be found to hold in any case where the prayer of faith is offered, but there is no doubt that it always holds good in cases where the strongholds of Satan are attacked, where the prey is to be wrested from the strong.

Think of the children of Israel under Joshua. God had given them the land of Canaan—*given* it to them, notice, by free grace—but see how they had to fight when once they commenced actually to take possession!

Satan's tactics seem to be as follows. He will first of all oppose our breaking through to the place of real, living faith by all means in his power. He detests the prayer of faith, for it is an authoritative "notice to quit." He does not so much mind rambling, carnal prayers, for they do not hurt him much. This is why it is so difficult to attain to a definite faith in God for a definite object. We often have to strive and wrestle in prayer (Eph. 6:10-12) before we attain this quiet, restful faith. And until we break right through and *join hands with God* we have not attained to real faith at all. Faith is a gift of God—if we stop short of it we are using mere fleshly energy or willpower, weapons of no value in this warfare. Once we attain to a real faith, however, all the forces of hell are impotent to annul it. What then? They retire and muster their forces on this plot of ground which God has pledged Himself to give us, and contest every inch of it. The real battle begins when the prayer of faith has been offered. But, praise the Lord! we are on the winning side. Let us read and re-read the tenth chapter of Joshua, and never talk about defeat again. Defeat, indeed! No. Victory! Victory! Victory!

Read 2 Samuel 23:8-23. All I have been saying is found in a nutshell in verses 11 and 12. Let Shammah represent the Christian warrior. Let David represent the crucified and risen Christ—and note that Shammah was one of the "mighty men whom David had." Let the "plot of ground" represent the prayer of faith. Let the lentils, if you will, represent the poor lost souls of men. Let the Philistines represent the hosts of wickedness. Let "the people" represent Christians afflicted with spiritual anemia.

I can imagine what these people were saying as they saw the Philistines approaching and ran away! "Perhaps it was not the Lord's will to grant us that plot of ground. We must submit to the will of God."

Yes, we must indeed submit ourselves to God, but we must also "resist the devil" (James. 4:7). The fact that the enemy comes upon us in force is no proof that we are out of the line of God's will. The constant prefixing of "if it be Thy will" to our prayers is often a mere subterfuge of unbelief. True submission to God is not inconsistent with virility and boldness. Notice what Shammah did—simply *held his ground*. He was not seeking more worlds to conquer at that moment! He just stood where he was and hit out right and left. Notice also the result of his action and to whom the glory is ascribed!

Now then, do it. 2 Samuel 3:18

"Try" is a word constantly in the mouth of unbelievers. "We must do what we can," they say. It is far too often taken up by believers. In our experience, "to try" has usually meant "to fail." The word of the Lord in reference to His various commands is not, "Do your best," but "Do it"; that is, do the thing commanded.

J. HUDSON TAYLOR, *God's Fellow Workers*

The Prayer of Faith - V

6. PRAYING THROUGH TO VICTORY. I repeat that this does not necessarily apply to every kind of prayer. A young Lisu Christian here is fond of telling an experience of his a few months ago. He was walking through the fields in the evening when his insides began unaccountably to pain him. He dropped on his knees and, bowing his head down to the ground, asked Jesus to cure him. At once the stomachache left him. Praise the Lord! And there are, no doubt, multitudes of such cases—simple faith and simple answers. But we must not rest content with such prayer. We must get beyond stomachache or any other ache, and enter into the deeper fellowship of God's purposes. "That ye be no longer children" (Eph. 4:14). We must press on to maturity. We must attain to "the measure of the stature of the fullness of Christ," and not remain in God's kindergarten indefinitely. If we grow into manhood in the spiritual life we shall not escape conflict. As long as Ephesians 6:10-18 remains in the Bible, we must be prepared for serious warfare—"and having done all, to stand." We must fight through, and then stand victorious on the battlefield.

Isn't this another secret of many unanswered prayers—that they are not fought through? If the result is not seen as soon as expected, Christians are apt to lose heart, and if it is still longer delayed to abandon it altogether.

We must count the cost before praying the prayer of faith. We must be willing to pay the price. We must mean business. We must set ourselves to "see things through" (Eph. 6:18, "with all perseverance"). Our natural strength will fail, and herein lies the necessity for a divinely given faith. We can then rest back in the Everlasting Arms and renew our strength continually. We can then rest as well as wrestle. In this conflict-prayer, after the definite exercise of faith, there is no need to ask the same thing again and again. It seems to me inconsistent to do so. Under these circumstances, I would say let prayer take the following forms:

(a) A firm *standing on God-given ground*, and a constant assertion of faith and claiming of victory. It is helpful, I find, to repeat passages of Scripture applicable to the subject. Let faith be continually strengthened and fed from its proper source—the Word of God.

(b) A definite fighting and *resisting of Satan's host* in the Name of Christ. I like to read passages of Scripture such as 1 John 3:8 or Rev. 12:11 in prayer as direct weapons against Satan. I often find it a means of much added strength and liberty in prayer to fight in this way. Nothing cuts like the Word of the living God (Heb. 4:12).

(c) *Praying through* every aspect of the matter in detail. In the case of my Lisu work here I continually pray to God to give me fresh knowledge of His will, more wisdom in dealing with the people, knowledge of how to pray, how to maintain victory, how to instruct the people in the gospel, or in singing or in prayer, help in studying the language, help in ordinary conversation, help in preaching, guidance as to settling down somewhere as a center, guidance about building a house (if necessary), guidance in my personal affairs (money, food, clothes, etc.), help and blessing in my correspondence, openings for the Word and blessing in other villages, for leaders and helpers to be raised up for me, for each of the Christians by name, also for every one of my prayer helpers by name. Such detailed prayer is exhausting, but I believe effectual in regard to ascertaining the will of God and obtaining His highest blessing.

I have set the Lord always before me. Psalm 16:8

Let us see to it that we keep God before our eyes; that we walk in His ways, and seek to please and glorify Him in everything, great and small. Depend on it, God's work, done God's way, will never lack God's supplies.

J. Hudson Taylor, *Dwelling In Him*

Prayer Dividends

Ten years had passed. The groundwork of prayer, faith, and patience was well laid in Lisuland. The steady plodding round and round that Jericho wall continued year after laborious year not only by Fraser himself but also by his faithful prayer forces at home. When would God's time come and the prayer of faith be fulfilled? Should Fraser stay on, waiting and praying, while other more responsive fields lay idle because of lack of harvesters?

The day came when Fraser felt that a time must be set. One more journey around the district from village to village where he was well known; then if the Lord did not indicate otherwise, he would offer for another field for a time—until the time for harvest came among the Lisu. He started out on that "last" journey. The response was the same dull apathy—or was it? As he set out early the second morning his host, who had been wholly non-committal the night before, declared that as a family they wanted to turn from their demon worship to God's way. Fraser could scarcely believe his ears. Others followed after this first family had made the break. All during that journey calls came from villages high up on the mountain side or deep down in the ravine or across the valley. Not only family after family but village after village made a public decision to turn from darkness to light, from the power of Satan to God. Was it too good to be true? No! The movement of God so long prayed for was gradually spreading throughout the area. God's time had come.

I BELIEVE it was January 12, 1915, that I was definitely led to ask God for "several hundreds of families" from the Lisu. Some may say, "Your prayer has at last been answered." No! I took the answer *then*. I believed *then* that I had it. The realization has only now come, it is true, but God does not keep us waiting for *answers*. He gives them *at once*. (Daniel 9:23)

I wish you could have been with me as I went from village to village, to have seen the royal reception they gave me! And you would have shared in it too. What with the playing of their bagpipes, the firing off of guns, the lining up of all the villagers, men and women, young and old, to shake hands with you (they use both hands, thinking it more respectful) you have a feeling of being over-whelmed—an "overweight of joy."

. . . .

Imagine what it is to have between five and six hundred families (representing some three thousand people) look-ing to you as father, mother, teacher, shepherd, and advis-er! It is a big responsibility.

I went in for big things when I took up tribes work and I do not regret it. I believe that to a large extent we get what we go in for with God—only sometimes we have mistaken ideas as to how it will come about. Rejoice with me and pray on for them all, in every phase of need you can think of.

. . . .

The people are perhaps shivering through their rags. They are poor, dirty, ignorant and superstitious, but they are *God's gift to us*. You ask God for spiritual children, and He chooses them out for you. You shake hands with the brothers and sisters and mothers He has found for you, and sit down with the boys and girls all around you. For I would rather teach Lisu children to sing "Jesus loves me, this I know" than teach integral calculus to the most intel-ligent student who has no interest in China.

Two things stand out clearly in my mind: first, how "foolish" and "weak" our new converts are; and second, that God has *really* chosen them. 1 Corinthians 1:27-28 is fulfilled before my very eyes! If you could come out here and see how useless mere preaching and persuasion is among these people, you would understand this better. One feels so helpless in face of their ignorance and need! But the Lisu work in our present district, with over two hundred families on either side of the Salween River (four hundred and more families in all), has been spontaneous from the beginning.

They will take you to a village you have never set foot in or even heard of before, and you will find several families of converts there, some of whom can now read and write after a fashion, and a chapel already put up! They just teach one another—inviting converts over from neighboring villages for that purpose. They just *want* to be Christians when they hear all about it and turn Christian, missionary or no missionary. Who put that "want-to" in their hearts? If they are not God's chosen, God's elect, what are they?

. . . .

I used to think that prayer should have the first place and teaching the second. I now feel it would be truer to give prayer the first, second, and third places, and teaching the fourth.

These people out here are not only ignorant and superstitious—they have a heathen atmosphere about them. One can actually feel it. We are not dealing with an enemy that fires at the head only—that keeps the mind only in ignorance—but with an enemy who uses poison gas attacks which wrap the people round with deadly effect, and yet are impalpable, elusive. What would you think of the folly of the soldier who fired a gun into the gas to kill it or drive it back? Nor would it be of any more avail to teach or preach to the Lisu here while they are held back by these invisible forces. Poisonous gas cannot be dispersed, I suppose, in any other way than by the wind springing up and dispersing it. Man is powerless.

But the breath of God can blow away all those miasmic vapors from the atmosphere of a village in answer to your prayers. We are not fighting against flesh and blood. You deal with the fundamental issues of this Lisu work when you pray against the principalities, the powers, the world rulers of this darkness, the spiritual hosts of wickedness in the heavenlies (Eph. 6:12).

I believe that a work of God sometimes goes on behind a particular man or family, village or district before the knowledge of the truth ever reaches them. It is a silent, unsuspected work, not in mind or heart, but in the unseen realm behind these. Then, when the light of the gospel is brought, there is no difficulty, no conflict. It is, then, simply a case of "Stand still and see the salvation of the Lord."

This should give us confidence in praying intelligently for those who are far from the gospel light. The longer the preparation, the deeper the work. The deeper the root, the firmer the plant when once it springs above ground. I do not believe that any deep work of God takes root without long preparation somewhere.

On the human side, evangelistic work on the mission field is like a man going about in a dark, damp valley with a lighted match in his hand seeking to ignite anything ignitable. But things are damp through and through and will not burn however much he tries. In other cases, God's wind and sunshine have prepared beforehand. The valley is dry in places, and when the lighted match is applied—here a shrub, there a tree, here a few sticks, there a heap of leaves take fire and give light and warmth long after the kindling match and its bearer have passed on. And this is what God wants to see, and what He will be inquired of us for: little patches of fire burning all over the world.

From Me is thy fruit found. Hosea 14:8

"I am the true Vine." The first two words, "I am," give us the key to the whole secret of fruitfulness. Not what we are, but what He is; not what we do, but what His life works in and through us is the question of the moment. "From Me is thy fruit found." He is the true Fruitbearer.

J. HUDSON TAYLOR, *Fruit Bearing*

PRAYER TOOLS

Will Bruce

Praying for One Another - I

Every Christian in our modern world is under constant satanic pressure and attack. We must bear one another's burdens as we see these pressures escalating. We can and must do this by regular, specific prayer. So much of our praying is limited to just, "Lord, bless ...," or, "Lord, meet the need of ..."

We are admonished in Galatians 6:2 to bear one another's burdens. Some burdens are too heavy to be borne alone. This happens because of a sudden flood of problems, a lack of adequate Bible teaching or because of spiritual immaturity. On the other hand, Galatians 6:5 tells us there are burdens for which each one must take responsibility. He must seek God's help and do what he can for himself. In 2 Corinthians 1:8-11, Paul writes of the extreme pressures that can be handled only through the prayers of others.

To be guilty of the sin of prayerlessness is to be guilty of the worst form of practical atheism. It is actually saying we can get along without His help while the evidence is very clear on every hand that we cannot. Could it be that the sin of prayerlessness stems from our unbelief that He is a living God who exercises direct influence on the affairs of men?

Instead of waiting until crisis problems develop which result in panic praying for others, we need to trust God to protect them as we pray Spirit-led, thoughtful, caring prayers before the problems overwhelm them and they are unable to cope. We need to engage in major battles, not just minor skirmishes, moving from surface praying to in-depth praying. We need to pray both defensively and offensively.

Praying for others is vital to our own spiritual growth. If we pray for them at all we often get bogged down with the material or the trivial and do not move on to the spiritual and the eternal. Where are our priorities? Often they are so clouded by humanistic and materialistic philosophies on the one hand and the pressures of the day on the other that we ignore the spiritual almost entirely. Needless to say, we do not cease to intercede for material needs as we learn to pray protectively for spiritual needs and growth. We need to progress beyond, "Lord, bless John and Mary," and be specific, thus moving from crisis praying to protective praying.

For example: Fred or Jane is unemployed. We pray for a job, as we should, but what is God saying in this circumstance? What are the spiritual lessons to be learned? What are the attitudes, the frustrations, the mental depressions, the fears? How about the interpersonal relationships within and outside the family? Is God glorified in this time of stress by their actions and reactions? Many times in our very limited intercession for others we pray for deliverance from difficult circumstance, sickness, or accident. We forget to ask that Fred or Jane will take God's more than ample provision and learn the lessons God has for both in this trial. Our concern is not necessarily for the removal of the problem but for victory in it and God's glory. Daniel was not kept out of the lion's den. He was kept in it!

Another example: After six years of seeing the happy marriage of a fine young couple who have been leading the young people's group, we find that they have filed for divorce on grounds of incompatibility. They say, "We no longer love each other." We petition God with deep concern for them in this crisis, but have we been praying for them protectively, strategically, specifically and with discernment during their years of married life?

As we recognize the absolute necessity of praying protectively for one another and bearing one another's burdens, we must not excuse ourselves by saying, "How can I pray for them when they do not tell me their needs?" Others' needs are often similar to our own. As we think of their needs, His Word and His Spirit will lead us in prayer.

Most gladly, therefore, will I rather glory in my infirmities.
2 Corinthians 12:9

Paul was distressed by a burden which he did not have strength to bear, and asked that the burden might be removed. God answered the prayer, not by taking it away, but by showing him the power and the grace to bear it joyfully. Thus that which had been the cause of sorrow and regret now became the occasion of rejoicing and triumph.

J. HUDSON TAYLOR, *When You Pray*

Praying for One Another - II

PRAY THAT THE ONE FOR WHOM WE ARE INTERCEDING:

... will realize his present exalted position in Christ.
Paul places the utmost importance on the child of God entering into a mature partnership with the Father. This is partially achieved by realizing his present exalted position before God in heaven now through the work of the Lord Jesus on the cross. It is only as we acknowledge who we really are in Christ that we can live this new identity. Many believers seem to be ignorant of this. Pray that others will get their true identity and self-worth from who they are in Christ and not from success, failure or what others say or think about them.

... will present himself as a living sacrifice.
In Romans 12:1,2 Paul presents the ultimate and totally necessary step of Christian dedication. This is presenting our bodies and all we have and are as a living sacrifice to God. This commitment is not essential to salvation, but no progress will be made in the Christian life without it. Pray that others, like Paul, will cry out, "Lord, what do You want me to do?" and then do it.

... will be filled with the Holy Spirit.
The Lord commands us to be filled (Ephesians 5:18). The filling of the Holy Spirit is not optional equipment for the Christian. Nothing in the spiritual life is accomplished without His power and in-filling. In the measure that we are not Spirit-filled we are self-centered, selfish and carnal. Pray that the believer will allow the Holy Spirit to work daily in his life.

... will be regular and systematic in the study of God's Word.

It is essential for us to pray specifically that the one we are praying for will take the Word of God as his food, guide, companion, only source of information about God and the spiritual life, only authority, and the ultimate fountain of joy in this life (Psalm 119). Pray, too, that as he is in the Word he will appropriate it and obey it, let God's Word guide him, show him his blind spots, and keep him balanced.

Let not that man think that he shall receive anything of the Lord. James 1:7

Only those prayers will be answered which are in harmony with the revealed will of God. Unless the word of God is abiding in us, how can we be sure that our petitions are in harmony with His will?

J. HUDSON TAYLOR, *When You Pray*

Praying for One Another - III

... will have the mind of Christ.

In 1 Corinthians 2:11-16 the spiritual man is seen as having both the spirit of man and the Spirit of God. Thus we pray for the believer, that having supernatural life in Christ through the indwelling Holy Spirit, he may appropriate the mind of Christ in all matters of life. Pray that he will choose to make Christlike decisions in regard to priorities, goals, and guidance, with sharpened insights so as not to waste time on good things and miss God's best. Pray that he will constantly live with eternity's values in view, an attitude impossible to attain without the realization that the Christian life is a miracle life from beginning to end (Galatians 3:1-3).

... will grow daily in Christian maturity.

Nothing is more tragic than a twenty-year-old infant! Many today are in that spiritual condition after having been saved for a number of years. Pray that the believer will see that after the crisis experience of being born again there is the lifelong process of daily growth in Christ that takes patience, time, discipline, and the power of the Holy Spirit (Ephesians 2:10; 4:11-16; Philippians 2:12 and 13). The mature Christian must have a spirit of forgiveness with no root of bitterness because of any treatment of himself or others. He must learn to handle stress, frustrations, and unfulfilled expectations in a Christlike manner.

... will appropriate the full armor of God.

Pray that the believer will have his eyes opened to the dangers of certain satanic attacks and will put on the full armor of God. The armor plus the skillful use of the authority he has in the victorious Christ insures full protection (Ephesians 6:10-18; Colossians 2:1-15). Pray that the one for whom we are praying will fulfill his responsibility as one born for battle, resist temptation and repent promptly of any sin in his life.

... will be alert to Satan's strategy.

Pray that the believer will not only be kept from sin but also that he will be aware of the threefold satanic temptations: the lust of the flesh (fulfilling any of our desires outside the will of God) is Satan's effort to get us out of the will of God; the lust of the eyes (coveting that which God does not allow at a particular time or place) is Satan's effort to get us to distrust God; the pride of life (self effort or independence from God) is Satan's effort to destroy our confidence in God (1 John 2:16). Also he must realize that he is incapable of meeting Satan in his own strength. Victory comes only as he takes the victory of Calvary as his own (1 Corinthians 15:57, 58). Pray that he will discern between satanic pressure and godly chastening, and remain keenly alert to all satanic deception.

He purgeth it, that it may bring forth more fruit. John 15:2

If we are purified, at times, as in a furnace, it is not merely for earthly sacrifice; it is for eternity. May you so appreciate the plans of the Master that you can triumphantly glory in the love that subjects you to such discipline, though the discipline itself is sharp and to the flesh hard to bear.

J. HUDSON TAYLOR, *Fruit Bearing*

Praying for One Another - IV

... will not love the world system.

Pray that the child of God will have mental, emotional, doctrinal and moral stability in a day in which the pressures from peer groups, the media, and the world are increasing in their opposition to biblical standards. The believer must know that love of the world is not consistent with loving God (1 John 2:15-17). Pray that he will realize that his love for God is expressed through obedience. (John 14:15, 21, 23)

... will have a spirit of brokenness and humility.

Pray that the believer's pride will be broken and that he will deal with his sins through repentance and seeking forgiveness. Psalm 51:17 says: "The sacrifices of God are a broken spirit; a broken and a contrite heart, O God, Thou wilt not despise." Pray for willingness to give and take, willingness to change, and willingness to see another's viewpoint. Pray that the believer will have an understanding spirit in place of a judgmental one. Pray that instead of looking for someone to blame in various situations he will be willing to say, "I am sorry," or "I was wrong."

... will have a servant's heart.

Pray this believer will be convinced of the Lord's desire for him: that he be a servant of God and of his brothers in Christ. (Mk. 10:44-45)

... will build a Scriptural family.

Pray that the one for whom you are praying will look neither to the world nor to carnal Christians but to the Word of God, and that he will fulfill his God-ordained place as head and spiritual leader of his home. Pray that his wife will be submissive and seek the Lord's approval as did Sarah when she called Abraham, "Master" (1 Peter 3:6). Pray that as parents they will be firm, yet loving, realizing the absolute necessity of being godly models for their children. Pray that the husband and wife will maintain a balance among family, ministry, and job responsibilities (Ephesians 5:14 to 6:4), that all in the family will love each other with agape love, seeking the highest good for each other, rather than demanding their rights. Pray for those who are single that they will look to the Lord for His choice of a life partner; or pray that their lives will glorify God as singles.

... will become an effective prayer warrior.
Pray that the believer will have a vital and effective prayer life from a clean heart. It is absolutely necessary to keep short accounts with God. "If I regard iniquity in my heart the Lord will not hear me" (Psalm 66:18). See also 1 John 1:9. Pray that his praying will be Biblically based, specific, consistent, steadfast in the Spirit, in faith, and with understanding.

For your sakes He became poor, that ye ... might be rich.
2 Corinthians 8:9

Pray that we may daily follow Him who took our nature that He might raise us to be partakers of the Divine nature. Pray that this principle of becoming one with the people, of willingly taking the lowest place, may be deeply inwrought in our souls and expressed in our behavior.

J. HUDSON TAYLOR, *When You Pray*

Praying for One Another - V

... will know God's hand on him in physical and material things.

Pray that the one you are praying for will have the measure of health that will best glorify God. Pray that when set aside by ill health he will learn the lessons God has for him and draw upon Divine resources. Pray also for safety in travel, financial provision in keeping with God's plan for him, and proper use of the time and money God entrusts to him.

... will engage in prayerful worship.

To truly worship is to truly serve. Pray that the believer will not be on a treadmill of activity, substituting that for time with the Lord in true worship. Pray, too, that he will learn to praise the Lord, that he will give thanks for who he is in Christ, for spiritual growth, and for the fact that "God is a living God, He has spoken in the Bible; He means what He says, and will do all He has promised." (J.H. Taylor)

... will be involved in an accountability team.

Pray that he will not be deceived into thinking that he can stand alone and grow spiritually. Pray that he will select a group, or at least one person who is spiritually mature and committed to walking with God, to whom he will be especially accountable and faithful in all areas of his life. Pray that this commitment will be characterized by openness, honesty and teachableness. Pray that above all he will recognize his accountability to God: "So then, everyone shall give an account of himself to God." (Romans 14:12)

... will reach out to the unsaved.

Pray that others will love the lost as the Lord Jesus does and will reach out to a lost and dying world with the message of salvation. The Lord loved the unlovely and the destitute; His disciples should do no less. This love will best be communicated to the lost by a sacrificial sharing of the good news of Christ, sharing of themselves, and at times sharing materially with the hungry and needy. Pray that as God reveals His will as to the type and place of service at home or abroad, those who are His own will respond without hesitation.

For me to live is Christ. Philippians 1:21

Has Christ become to us such a living, bright reality that no post of duty is tedious, that as His witnesses we can return to the quiet homeside, or to the distant service, with hearts more than glad, more than satisfied, even if stripped of earthly friends and treasures?

J. HUDSON TAYLOR, *God's Fellow Workers*

Praying for One Another - VI

SO THEN, HOW DO WE PRAY FOR ONE ANOTHER?

- Confess sin and let the blood of Jesus cleanse. Prayer must flow from a cleansed vessel. Psalm 66:18, "If I regard iniquity in my heart the Lord will not hear me."
- Be tied to the mind of Christ so thoroughly that you think His thoughts about His embattled saints.
- Be motivated by love for God and a desire to help others (Hebrews 6:10, *NIV*).
- Pray fervently to be led by the Holy Spirit to the exact needs of the one for whom you ARE praying.
- Be specific, systematic, and steadfast in praying for others.
- Agree in prayer with others, the "two or three" of Matt. 18:19-20.
- Learn to saturate a situation or problem with prayer.
- Pray with the authority you have in Christ to bind the power of Satan. (Matthew 18:18, Mark 3:27).
- Pray the prayer of faith and claim the victory (1 Corinthians 15: 57-58.)
- Pray for others as you pray for yourself. Any problem you have others probably have, even if in a slightly different form.
- Use a passage of Scripture as you pray for others. Here are some suggestions: Ephesians 1:15-23; Colossians 1:9-12; Ephesians 3:14-21. (Use Scripture also in praying for yourself.)

ACCEPT YOUR RESPONSIBILITY

May you accept your responsibility of interceding for others by getting down to the real business of praying for them. "O God, awaken us all to our responsibility to pray for one another so that all Christians may glorify You and fulfill the purpose for which we have been saved!"

My voice shalt Thou hear in the morning, O Lord.
Psalm 5:3

Do not have your concert first, and then tune your instruments afterwards. Begin the day with the Word of God and prayer, and get first of all into harmony with Him.

J. HUDSON TAYLOR, *When You Pray*

Why and How to Pray for Missionaries - I

Why do we say: "Brothers and sisters, pray for us"? There are many reasons, including those listed below. The full-time missionary must have the intercessory missionary (prayer partner) working with him on a regular, systematic basis. We cannot work independently in the salvation, discipling, and training of national leaders. (2 Cor. 10:4)

THE MISSIONARY IS INVADING ENEMY TERRITORY. In most instances, Satan has held uncontested sway for centuries or even millenniums in the countries which we think of as "foreign mission fields." As a result, the thinking of the people is twisted, their minds are blinded, and God's truth does not penetrate easily. Satan does not meekly give up his prey; he counter-attacks in all and many times undreamed-of ways. He fights to the last ditch. We are in the midst of a spiritual battle. Intercessory missionaries must see themselves as part of the same team. (2 Cor. 10:4)

Pray that souls will be released from Satan's bondage and will put their trust in Christ. Pray that the missionary will recognize the attacks of the Adversary and use Scriptural weapons in the battle.

THE MISSIONARY FACES MANY FRUSTRATIONS. There is much to discourage and frustrate the missionary, such as:

Language Disparity. This means that we cannot clearly communicate the message of God's salvation until we have spent months or even years in language study.

Customs and Culture. These are often different, and sometimes conflict with our Western ways of doing things. But we are guests in these countries and must learn to be careful not to offend by thoughtlessly ignoring things that are important to those we have come to reach with the gospel.

Unfamiliar Food. These can be delicious or unpalatable. We have to subordinate our own tastes, and be prepared to eat what is offered if friendly relationships are to be established.

Climate. We who come from temperate zones often have problems adjusting to the tropics: enervating heat coupled with high humidity, typhoons and rainy season's deluges.

Lack of Privacy. Many people in other countries live much of their lives in public and expect the missionary to do the same. We must work out a balance.

Lack of Results when we expected to set the world on fire. There must be a constant "looking to Jesus."

Pray for the missionary to be graciously flexible and able in very practical ways to obey the injunction of Philippians 4:6 (worry about nothing, pray about everything).

In everything ... let your requests be made known to God.
Philippians 4:6

The Lord's will is that His people should be strong, healthy and happy. Shall we not determine to be "careful for nothing, but in everything by prayer and supplication with thanksgiving" bring those things that would become burdens or anxieties to God in prayer and live in His perfect peace?

J. Hudson Taylor, *When You Pray*

Why and How to Pray for Missionaries - II

THE MISSIONARY HAS NEED OF SELF-KNOWLEDGE. It is not long before we are again forced to face up to the fact of our own sinful flesh. We then recognize afresh how human we are! It's rough to learn what we are really like. Pressure will reveal it all too clearly! Here are a few of the revelations the Lord brings to our attention:

Pride of Race, which may be quite unintentional, yet is apparent to the national; pride of "face" and love of position or "place" may also be found.

Prejudice. "My" way and the way "I" have been taught is viewed as the only right way.

Selfishness. Lack of consideration for others, wanting attention, stubbornness, and the inability to see another's viewpoint can all come from this root of self.

Lack of Self-discipline. It is so easy to waste precious time, our own and others', on the mission field. We may also find that we do not have sufficiently defined, measurable goals for the work and insufficiently detailed programs for accomplishing them.

Pray that the missionary will learn to submit his own desires and inclinations to God's Holy Spirit, and then that the fruit of the Spirit will be more and more apparent in the life of the missionary. Pray that he will understand and appropriate all he has and is in Christ.

THE MISSIONARY FACES LONELINESS. It is easy to succumb to loneliness in a foreign land when we are surrounded by people of another culture and language. This is true of those who are single and those who are married. We all need to know we are loved and accepted. Loneliness is one of the means the devil uses to discourage and depress us and to cause us to engage in disastrous self-pity. But God has supplied a way of escape! His promise in Hebrews 13:5b, "I will never leave thee nor forsake thee," is as true today as it was when He first gave it. What we need to do is to claim it for ourselves and experience the presence of the Lord Jesus Christ in our everyday living.

Pray that the missionary will experience fellowship with God in new and satisfying ways.

THE MISSIONARY MUST REMEMBER THE MEANING OF BEING A MISSIONARY. It has been in our Bibles all the time, and on the field we really need to learn the truth of Christ's statement in John 6:38; "I have come down from heaven, not to do My own will, but the will of Him who sent Me" and Mark 10:45: "For even the Son of Man did not come to be served, but to serve, and to give His life a ransom for many." Our mission is to be servants to all. We are God's instruments, to be used as He sees fit. We must learn to work as team members regardless of our training, or talents, or lack of either.

Pray that the missionary will have the humility of Christ as described in Philippians 2:5-8.

They made me the keeper of the vineyards, but mine own vineyard have I not kept. **Song of Solomon 1:6**

If we are not watchful over the souls of others, and neglect our own—if we are seeking to remove motes from our brother's eye, unmindful of the beam in our own, we shall often be disappointed with our own powerlessness to help our brethren while our Master will not be less disappointed in us.

J. HUDSON TAYLOR, *God's Fellow Workers*

Why and How to Pray for Missionaries - III

THE MISSIONARY'S NEED FOR STABILITY. In all areas of life we must maintain equilibrium. Spiritually, there must be doctrinal stability through the study of the Bible and its application to our daily living. Mentally, we must learn how to combat Satan's great tool of depression. Emotionally, we need to strike a happy balance between becoming too calloused or too sympathetic.

Pray that in each of these areas the missionary will develop mature stability. Pray that the missionary will get his true identity and self-worth from who he is in Christ and not from success or what others think or say about him.

THE MISSIONARY'S INSIGHT NEEDS TO BE SHARPENED. We need insight into the heart-needs of those around us, both nationals and fellow missionaries to diagnose and to apply remedies. We need insight into methods of work in order to know what will best accomplish the task. We need insight concerning our priorities and the setting of goals. Once we acquire a working knowledge of the language, we need real wisdom from God to know which opportunities to pursue and which to leave undone.

Pray that the missionary will have a heightened sympathy and insight into the heart-needs of those around him. Pray, too, that he will have insight and heavenly wisdom to know what God would have him undertake, and how He would have him go about it.

THE MISSIONARY NEEDS GOOD INTERPERSONAL RELATIONSHIPS. These are all-important if God's work is to go forward unhindered. The oil of the Spirit of God must be operative to insure that we get along well with others: husband/wife, worker/co-worker, worker/director, worker/ national Christian, worker/national unbeliever. If relationships become strained we need to be honest and open with each other, show real repentance, and allow God to break our stubborn pride. It is no easier for us to admit we are wrong than for anyone else! Pray that in this important area the missionary will be surrendered to God and sensitive to the prompting of the Holy Spirit.

Pray that he will see his own personal needs. And that couples would love each other with agape love seeking the highest good rather than claiming their rights.

Until the Spirit be poured upon us from on high. Isaiah 32:15

Our God is an Almighty Savior, and my hope is in Him. If His Spirit is poured out, evil will be kept in check. If we ask for it, will it not truly be so? Let us pray then, often, for this, that division and discord may not prevail instead of unity and love.

J. Hudson Taylor, *When You Pray*

Why and How to Pray for Missionaries - IV

THE MISSIONARY'S NEED TO BE FILLED WITH THE SPIRIT. The Spirit's gracious fruit must show in our lives, or our work will accomplish nothing. Unless we have daily communion with our Lord, the pressure will result in failure, and we will finally drop from foreign service. We must keep spiritually fresh if we are to glorify Him.

Pray that the missionary will be able to obey the injunction of Ephesians 5:18; Galatians 5:16,25 ("Be filled with the Spirit ..." and therefore, walk in the Spirit) and that he will always keep short account with God (1 John 1:9), be aware of Satan's deceptions and hate all sin.

THE MISSIONARY'S HEALTH PROBLEMS. Physical health is important, and many workers have been disqualified for service on the grounds of ill health. Common foes are malaria, hepatitis, amoebic dysentery, and dengue fever. Excessive fatigue may cause depression or discouragement, with disastrous results in other areas. We need, too, to be aware of attacks upon our mental health. Our enemy sometimes attacks our minds, leading to mental and emotional problems. Anxiety and worry will soon drain us of all vitality. We need to learn to guard against these with the "shield of faith."

Pray that God will keep the missionary in that condition of health that will best glorify Him.

THE MISSIONARY'S TRAVEL. Travel on the field is very often hazardous, whether by plane, bus, car or on foot. Sometimes as we send up a quick prayer to God, we wonder if anyone else was led to pray at that moment.

Pray for safety in travel.

THE MISSIONARY'S CHILDREN. Our sons and daughters can be of the greatest blessing and help to us, or may pose a problem. Sometimes decisions made because of our children have a far-reaching effect on our lives or service, and theirs, too. Sadly, children that are loved but not disciplined can adversely affect our work and testimony. We need wisdom to train and teach them in ways well-pleasing to God and in full accordance with His Word.

Pray for the health of missionary children. Pray that both parents will be godly role models and will do all they can to help their children develop godly self-worth. Pray that parents may have wisdom in providing for their education. Pray that children, as well as parents, will have a good understanding and attitude if separation should become necessary for schooling. Pray especially that the children will not let any bitterness take root because of separation.

How much more shall your Heavenly Father give ... to them that ask Him. Luke 11:13

The many blessings enjoyed even by those who know Him not are still given and continued by His grace; and how much more may the children of this Heavenly Father look to Him with confidence, knowing that He will supply their every need in life, in death, and in the world to come!

J. HUDSON TAYLOR, *When You Pray*

Why and How to Pray for Missionaries - V

THE MISSIONARY'S CONSTANT NEED TO SHOW LOVE.
Love is required at all times, in all circumstances, for all people. Our human love will not do; it always falls short. Only the love of God which is "shed abroad" in our hearts by the Holy Spirit, and has the characteristics outlined in 1 Corinthians 13, will suffice.

Pray for the missionary as Paul prayed in Philippians 1:9 (that love "may abound more and more in knowledge and in all depth of insight"). Pray that at all times, in all circumstances, with all people, we will take that which God has so fully and freely provided. "God has given ... TAKE."

SHARE THE MISSIONARY'S BURDEN FOR ADDITIONAL WORKERS, BOTH NATIONAL AND FOREIGN. With untold millions dying untold and untaught millions dying untaught, plus the population explosion and the closing of doors, we must have more co-workers to gather in the harvest and disciple those who are coming to Christ.

Pray that many more at home and on the foreign field will make "His last command their first concern."

THE MISSIONARY'S OWN INTERCESSORY LIFE.
Missionaries must take time to pray for every aspect of the work in which they are engaged because they are so intimately involved in the local situation.

Pray that the missionary will recognize and faithfully fulfill his part in prayer for the work.

HOW DO YOU PRAY FOR MISSIONARIES?

- Be specific, systematic and steadfast.
- Agree in prayer with others. Matthew 18:19-20.

- Practice saturation praying—covering many aspects with many brief requests.
- Pray as for yourself. Any problem you have, the missionary may also have, but it will be magnified by his situation and circumstances.
- Pray with the authority you have in Christ, and bind the strong man. Matthew 18:18, Mark 3:27.
- Try using a passage of Scripture when you are praying for your missionary, such as Ephesians 1:15-23, Colossians 1:9-14, or Ephesians 3:16-21.

"Someone has said: 'Better, far better, do less work, if need be, in order that we may pray more; because work done by the rushing torrent of human energy will not save a single soul: whereas work done in vital and unbroken contact with the living God will tell for all eternity.' No doubt, we would all heartily agree with this—the trouble, of course, is to actually put it into practice."

The Lord called Moses up to the top of the mount.
Exodus 19:20

We must get on to a higher plane of thought altogether, and of prayer, if we are to walk worthy of God. Don't we want to truly meditate on God more, to gaze on Him, take in what we can take in of His greatness, His resources, His assurances and promises? Dwelling on Him in this way, shouldn't we be enabled to grasp more of the heights and depths of His character and purposes, and be more ready and able to do His will?

J. HUDSON TAYLOR, *When You Pray*

How to Pray for Missionaries' Kids (MKs) - I

When God calls Christians into ministry, He desires the whole family to be part of His witness in the community they serve. Strong Christian families can endure hardships, overcome difficulties, persevere in the face of discouragements, and be a powerful witness of God's love and grace through their daily lives. Unfortunately, Satan is also aware that one of his most effective strategies in hindering the Lord's work is to destroy the witness of the family by taking advantage of the vulnerability of children.

Missionaries' kids are extremely important members of the missionary team although often not recognized as such. Effective, strategic, knowledgeable prayer on their behalf can prevent the significant loss caused by their not adjusting to God's will for them.

Spiritual Life and Maturing

As with every individual, MKs must personally acknowledge Christ as Lord and Savior. The MKs' #1 priority must be to establish their true personal identity in Christ. Only then can they grow and mature in Christ.

Pray that MKs will have a personal relationship to Christ and put Him first in their lives, maintain a vital devotional life, and have a thankful attitude, while still not denying difficulties or griefs. Pray that they will be teachable and willing to accept spiritual guidance from parents, dorm parents and others, so that they will grow up secure, well adjusted and having a self-image based on who they are in Christ, able to remind themselves that Christ lives in them, fully assured of their salvation, and not pitying themselves because they are MKs. Like all children, MKs are seeking personal worth and success which is usually found through encouragement from their parents.

Pray that the MKs will recognize the skills they have as valuable; that they will have courage to pursue their interests; that the parents will positively reinforce the children's good behavior and encourage development of transferable skills; that MKs will at all times keep their priorities in line with the mind and the will of God; that their self-worth will be based on being children of God and not on human success.

We have no might ... but our eyes are upon Thee.
2 Chronicles 20:12

I myself, for instance, am not specially gifted, and am shy by nature, but my gracious and merciful God and Father inclined Himself to me, and when I was weak in faith He strengthened me while I was still young. He taught me in my helplessness to rest on Him, and to pray even about little things in which another might have felt able to help himself.

J. HUDSON TAYLOR, *God's Fellow Workers*

How to Pray for MKs - II

Family Dynamics

Sometimes lack of stability in missionary families can come from: (1) Failure of each family member to appropriate or understand their position in Christ or to be constantly alert to the deceptive attacks of Satan. (2) Long separations. (3) Rootlessness due to frequent moves. (4) Disunity and poor relationships within the family. (5) Failure to feel part of the ministry and consequent resentment when there are necessary separations. (6) A sense of neglect when letter writing is left to only one parent. (7) Failure to balance responsibilities toward ministry and family, resulting in the MKs feeling neglected.

Pray that missionary parents will make their children feel a part of their ministry; that parents of MKs will provide the love and attention their children need; that parents will balance ministry and family needs; that the MKs will learn the value of the parents' ministry; that parents (especially fathers) will spend quality time with each child one-on-one and with the family alone.

Dealing with Losses and Relationships

Due to constant changes and moves MKs may "lose" friends and have to cultivate new friendships much more often than their peers at home. Some grow reluctant to establish meaningful relationships and withdraw in despair. MKs need a sense of stability. The parents need sensitivity to any potential confusion in their children.

Pray that the MKs will accept the challenge of separation if it is necessary to live away from their parents, and will have courage to face loneliness and fears; that they will know it's okay to cry or be sad or lonely, but be sure of God's promise to "never leave them nor forsake them" (Hebrews 13:5). Pray they will form close healthy relationships and mutually supportive friendships with both nationals and their peers; that they will be protected from any who would wrongly influence their thinking; that the MKs will find good mentors; and that they will feel free to openly discuss problems, doubts and confusion. Pray that MKs will reach out to others who need friends, too; that prayer partners will be faithful in praying for them as well as for their parents. When families return for furlough or home assignment, the MK is exposed to new people, unfamiliar places, different culture and expectations, and thus also needs prayer in these areas. MKs need prayer for grace to relate to the many visitors in their homes as well as to those who host them.

I will be the God of all the families of Israel. Jeremiah 31:1

I do not believe that our Heavenly Father will ever forget His children. I am a very poor father, but it is not my habit to forget my children. God is a very, very good Father. It is not His habit to forget His children.

J. HUDSON TAYLOR, *Great Is Thy Faithfulness*

How to Pray for MKs - III

Personal Standards

The MKs must develop godly principles and standards. They will need to be firmly grounded in God's Word and develop their own values based upon it. The MKs need to adopt and maintain high Biblical values in order to enable them to resist godless circumstances and pressure from their peers, the media and Satan. MKs must be taught to accept themselves, their bodies, their urges, as part of God's plan. Healthy sexuality must be positively taught, first in the parents' acceptance of themselves, and then in parents initiating healthy discussions appropriate to the needs of the kids.

Pray that the MKs, if subjected to destructive temptations such as drugs, alcohol, sex, pornography, and unedifying movies and videos, will resist them and set good examples for weaker peers; that when Satan tempts them they will resist him (James 4:7) and claim their position in Christ. Pray that they will view themselves as God's creation and walk in the light with Jesus in all relationships.

The Lord shall preserve thy going out and thy coming in.
Psalm 121:8

We must trust in Him; therefore we must seek to do His will. Preserved by Him, we are as safe in the tempest as in the calm, on sea as on shore, beneath an eastern sky as in much-loved England. Without His protection we are safe nowhere, with it we are safe anywhere and everywhere.

J. HUDSON TAYLOR, *Great Is Thy Faithfulness*

How to Pray for MKs - IV

Cultural Adjustment

There is the continuing trauma of not quite belonging anywhere. When the MK is serving with his parents, he is singled out as a foreigner, but when he returns to the so-called "home country" he may not feel at home and may have difficulty fitting in. The MK needs to accept or at least tolerate different ways and customs and be willing to adapt. Language may also be a problem. Being able to cope is a great challenge to the MK.

Pray that the MKs will have an appreciation for the unique experiences they have had and that they might see how future ministry or vocation can be enriched by these experiences. Pray that the parents will help their children see their lives in a broad, global sense, encouraging them to consider ministry, whether at home or abroad, while being very careful not to put undue pressure on them, realizing that the Holy Spirit, through the Scriptures, must lead them individually.

For Physical Safety and Health

Disasters such as typhoons, volcanoes, earthquakes, floods, drought, fires, as well as murders, kidnapping, robbery, unstable governments and hazardous travel, threaten many missionary families. Many underdeveloped countries have very high pollution or lack adequate medical care or nutritious foods, causing some families to leave the field because of illness.

Pray that when MKs experience crisis situations their trust in God will not be shaken. Pray for safety. Pray for the measure of health that will best glorify our Lord. Pray for protection from indigenous and common diseases and that the MKs and their parents will remember that the only really safe place is in the will of God.

danger, of man's approval or disapproval, in no way affect our duty. Should circumstances arise involving us in what may seem special danger, I trust we shall have grace to manifest the reality and depth of our trust in Him, and prove we are followers of the Good Shepherd who did not flee from death itself.

J. HUDSON TAYLOR, *God's Fellow Workers*

How to Pray for MKs - VI

Finances

Many MKs have been raised on limited financial resources (by home-side standards), yet may have lived in very undeveloped countries where they may even have felt rich. This dichotomy has an effect on the MKs' view of wealth.

Pray they will accept their financial status without assuming attitudes of "the world owes me a living" because their families have been supported by others; that MKs will not become bitter at the lack of "things" while growing up; and that financial limitations will not cause them to make personal wealth their life goal.

Education and Development

MKs may not realize that their education on the field is often superior to that in their home countries, and that their cross-cultural experience is an education in itself.

Pray for homeschooled MKs: for protection of their study hours from undue interruption; arrival of their study materials in good time and condition; self-discipline for mothers in patiently holding children to their prescribed work; friendships outside the home; and the extra pressure on the mother.

Pray for MKs living at home and attending local national or international schools for: ability to keep up with classmates where possible or to accept themselves if they fall behind.

Pray regarding mission schools, that God will give special wisdom for mission leadership in regard to personnel who teach and care for the MKs, and wisdom in carefully supervising the school personnel.

Pray that MKs who are in a boarding school will adjust, get along with the house parents and other MKs, and look to the Lord when struck with homesickness. Pray that the caregivers will have godly wisdom to care for the spiritual and emotional as well as educational and physical needs of the MKs. Pray for MKs who have concerns, fears and anxieties about the future, regarding their careers, further schooling, life partner, etc.

Pray that the MKs will have assurance that the Lord will adequately meet their academic, social, school, emotional, and physical needs just as He is able to meet all their spiritual needs. Pray that the MKs will be protected from psychological, physical and sexual abuse in every situation.

When I sent you ... lacked ye anything? They said, Nothing.
Luke 22:35

It has been wonderful and beautiful to see how the Lord has helped us ... Our hearts have been kept in peace, knowing that God's promises cannot fail; and to the question, "Lacked ye anything?" we can only reply as did the disciples of old, "Nothing, Lord."

J. HUDSON TAYLOR, *God's Guiding Hand*

How to Pray for MKs - VII

Reentry to the Home Country

Most MKs reenter their home country after completing high school. Proper reentry is crucial to the MKs as they enter adulthood. They need to find a campus support group, an extended family and friends, and a supportive church, especially if they are not living with their relatives. It is important that they attend a reentry seminar if at all possible to assist in the adjustment to a lifestyle that will often be different from the one with which they grew up.

Pray for good self-images rooted in their relationship with God, that will not be threatened by cultural adjustments. Pray for keen observation skills; for a desire to know and understand others; for courage to ask appropriate questions; and for a special friend to whom they can go for information and clarification. MKs often view the home-country kids as self-centered, affluent, shallow, living in a fast-paced environment and unaware of the rest of the world. Pray that, rather than becoming cynical, the MKs will prayerfully choose their standards based on God's Word and will not judge those around them. Pray that they will demonstrate godly priorities and principles and influence others for Christ.

Pray that MKs will not be proud or withdraw in disappointment, but realize that the majority of their new friends have not had the opportunity to see the world as they have. Pray that God will give them boldness in sharing the things they have witnessed and the ways they have seen Him work, and that they will take the challenge to inform and expose the church to world needs and not expect everyone to be excited about their lives and experiences as MKs.

Accept Your Responsibility

Effective, strategic, specific and regular prayer for MKs is absolutely essential. Missionaries do their part in fulfilling

will have the grace to receive criticism and profit by it, and that he will have a servant's heart. Pray that he will cultivate true humility in his walk, depending on God, not on his education, methods or personality, that he would always pray and wait on God's leading and timing and then in both his successes and his failures, in all things, that he will be careful to give God all the glory. Pray against pride so that he will remain useable.

Stability
Since we live in this carnal world with all its open and hidden pressures, pray that your pastor will keep his eyes on the Lord and serve with singleness of heart and will not become conceited over success or depressed by failure. Pray he will remember that Christians "march to a different drum," that our value system is different from that of the world.

Relationships
Pray that your pastor will know how to deal with his own frustrations, with the lack of gifts in certain areas, with well-meaning but stubborn people in his congregation, and that he will walk in true brokenness, for it is no easier for a pastor to say, "I am wrong," or "I am sorry," than it is for anyone else. Pray that he will be patient with himself and others as he fulfills his varied responsibilities, that Calvary love will be shown in all interpersonal relationships and that he will sense the love and support of his congregation.

Joy
Pray that your pastor will find real joy in his ministry in spite of spiritual struggles and problems. (John 16:24; 17:13) Joy is a significant hallmark of being filled with the Spirit—joy, great joy and peace, in the midst of and despite all circumstances. (2 Cor. 4:7-18, James 1:2-4, 1 Peter 1:6-9, Eph. 5:18-21)

Health
Pray for your pastor's health and the lessons God will teach

him in his time of sickness and recovery—resting in God's will and timing. Pray that he will maintain balance in exercise and recreation. Intercede, too, for safety as he travels.

Self Discipline

Since the pastor must prioritize and guard his time, be disciplined, and learn to say "no," pray that the Holy Spirit will make him sensitive in these matters and that he will deal with role conflicts and stress in the Spirit and not in the flesh which results in "burnout." (Matthew 11:30)

Our sufficiency is of God. **2 Corinthians 3:5**

The work is always increasing; and were it not for the consciousness of Christ as my life, hour by hour, I could not go on. But He is teaching me glorious lessons of His sufficiency, and each day I am carried onward with no feeling of strain, or fear of collapse.

J. HUDSON TAYLOR, *God's Fellow Workers*

Pastors Need Prayer Too - II

FAMILY NEEDS

Family Relationships

A pastor and his family live a kind of "fish-bowl" lifestyle. Therefore God's people need to respect the time they need as a family, and to pray that husband and wife will be devoted to one another and will be deeply related to each other, that the pastor will maintain a scriptural family seeking God's wisdom for the discipline of his children. Pray also for balance in time and attention given his wife and children as he strives to provide good spiritual leadership for them.

Pressures

Pointed prayer is needed as your pastor and his family face daily temptations, stresses, peer pressures, and satanic attacks because they are special targets of the enemy. On the other hand, pray church leaders will recognize the personal, spiritual, physical, material and social needs of the pastor and his family so that they may not need to become overly preoccupied with the affairs of this life. (2 Tim. 2: 3-4; 1 Tim. 5:17-18)

Whereby are given unto us exceeding great and precious promises. 2 Peter 1:4

Like air and light, equally needful in every clime and in every circumstance, the promises and assurances of God's precious Word meet us with help and comfort in all our various surroundings. It is our Father's will that His children shall be absolutely without worries.

J. HUDSON TAYLOR, *Great Is Thy Faithfulness*

Pastors Need Prayer Too - III

SPIRITUAL NEEDS

Spiritual Freshness

Pray that your pastor will "walk in the light" with Jesus daily and depend on the Spirit's power in all phases of his life and ministry. Because his hardest job will be to keep spiritually fresh, pray that the pastor always remembers these facts concerning spiritual vitality: (1) the ministry is spiritual warfare, not just a job or a profession; (2) life's pressures will always result in spiritual decline unless he is careful to maintain a close walk with the Lord; (3) his need for spiritual enlightenment. Pray he continues to grow in Christ-like maturity, realizing who he is in Christ, keeping short accounts with God.

Prayer

Pray that your pastor will understand that prayer is an absolute necessity and that he will prioritize his prayer life despite his very busy schedule. Over one hundred years ago, Lord Cecil said, "The greatest menace to ministerial usefulness crouches at the door of the secret place." Pray that your pastor will model an effective prayer life.

Integrity

Pray that he will resist moral temptation in line with who he is and Whom he serves—the Holy God, that his words and his actions will set a godly example and also that his thought-life will glorify God, and not pave the way for him and others to fall into immorality.

Spiritual Warfare

Above all, pray that your pastor will appropriate the full armor of God as outlined in Ephesians 6:10-18, being constantly aware of Satan's strategy at all times. Pastors are subject to the three-fold satanic temptation of the lust of the flesh, the lust of the eyes, and the pride of life, just as everyone else (1 John 2:16). Pray that he will continually realize victory comes only through Christ, that he have the Word hidden in his heart and his armor on at all times and know how to use the Sword of the Spirit in dealing with satanic opposition, oppression and possession.

Accountability

Pray that God will bless him with church leaders to whom he is accountable and that he will cultivate the friendship of at least one godly man (in or out of his congregation) to whom he will be especially open, transparent and spiritually accountable in all areas of his life and ministry. Pray that he will be keenly aware of the effects of his actions on the testimony of our Lord, on the church at large, on his own flock, as well as on his family and himself and, above all, aware of his accountability to God.

———

Worthy is the Lamb ... to receive ... glory and blessing.
Revelation 5:12

Do we sufficiently cultivate this unselfish desire to be all for Jesus, and to do all for His pleasure? Or are we conscious that we principally go to Him for our own sakes, or at best for the sake of our fellow creatures? How much of prayer there is that begins and ends with the creature, forgetful of the privilege of giving joy to the Creator.

J. HUDSON TAYLOR, *When You Pray*

Pastors Need Prayer Too - IV

CONGREGATIONAL NEEDS

Pulpit Preparation

Since God's Word and His Spirit do the lasting work in the church, pray that your pastor will give priority to study of the Word and to prayer. Study in sermon preparation must not be a substitute for personal communion with God nor for a time of private worship. Lord Cecil also said, "The greatest defect in the pastor's life is the lack of the devotional habit." Pray for a prepared pastor as well as a prepared sermon, that his messages will not reflect human pressures but only the leading of the Holy Spirit, that the pastor will give a balanced presentation of Scripture and not go off on tangents, and that he will present missions and evangelism as God's heart emphasizes in the Scriptures.

Christ-Centered and Christ-Exalting Preaching

Pray that the pastor's preaching will be "less of me and more of Christ" (Gal. 2:20) to edify the people and increase their love for Jesus and devotion to our Savior. Pray that through it, God will show them how to develop a life of worship, and he will emphasize the need to go home and feed themselves.

Fruitful Relationships

Pray that in all his relationships the pastor will be discerning, open, flexible, understanding, and forgiving, that he will be patient and that he will make himself available to his people. Pray he will have a heart of compassion, be a good listener balancing tenderness with wisdom, and firmness with love.

Individual Growth

Pray that with boldness, tenderness and love, your pastor will uncompromisingly confront sin. Pray his words will be loving, but firm and that the people will respond to the conviction of the Holy Spirit. Pray that he will preach for a response in changed lifestyles, that individuals will become progressively more Christ-like and not merely add to their store of biblical knowledge, and that the pastor will deal with anything in his own life that is not in line with who he is and Whom he serves. (Matt. 18: 15-35)

Mobilization

Also, pray that your pastor will encourage God's people in all the various stages of Christian growth and will help them discover their spiritual gifts by stepping out to fill a need. Pray that God will equip His people to train disciples and that the pastor will be absolutely committed to mobilizing the gifts of the body.

Discernment

Pray for your pastor to have discernment in all areas including: (1) how to apply God's Word to specific situations; (2) how to present biblical truth so that it will be understood and put into practice; and (3) how to rightly assess and utilize the abilities and gifts of others. In view of the excessive demands on his time, pray that he will have discernment as to what God wants him to do and how God wants it done. Human discernment is always inadequate, but the mind of Christ is the sole judge for deciding what to say or do in all matters and actions, "That nothing be done out of selfish ambition or vain conceit." (Philippians 2:3-8 NIV) Pray for stability in the pastor's life, since it is so easy to be swayed by trends, fads, and by winds of doctrine, and that he will keep balanced in all things. Pray that he will emphasize the need for all ages in the congregation to be united in love as God's family.

Counseling

Furthermore, pray that your pastor will not abandon his God-given right and responsibility to counsel his people in the wisdom of the Holy Spirit from the Word of God and call them to repent from and deal with any sin in their lives. Pray that he will not feel that psychology and "how-to programs" rather than the Bible, have the answers for today's troubled souls.

A FURTHER SUGGESTION

As you pray for your pastor you will discover that your hearts are knit together in a common purpose. You will understand that he, like Elijah, is "a man, just like us" yet he is the man who has been appointed by the Holy Spirit as your pastor (Acts 20:28). Don't pray "at him," but for him, and as you do, you will experience the marvelous way in which the Holy Spirit will bring to your mind special needs about which you should pray.

Finally, should you experience frustration in praying for your pastor, study and use the prayers of the Apostle Paul; they give much fuel for prayer. Please note: Ephesians 1:15-23, 3:14-21; Philippians 1:9-11; 2 Thessalonians 1:11-12 and 2 Corinthians 1:9-11.

"For this reason, since the day we heard about you, we have not stopped praying for you and asking God to fill you with the knowledge of His will through all spiritual wisdom and understanding. And we pray this in order that you may live a life worthy of the Lord and may please Him in every way: bearing fruit in every good work, growing in the knowledge of God, being strengthened with all power according to His glorious might so that you may have great endurance and patience, and joyfully giving thanks to the Father, who has qualified you to share in the inheritance of the saints in the kingdom of light." (Colossians 1:9-12, *NIV*)

Behold I have set before thee an open door. Revelation 3:8

Let but devoted laborers be found, who will prove faithful to God, and there is no reason to fear that God will not prove faithful to them. He will set before them an open door, and will esteem them of more value than the sparrows and the lilies that He clothes and feeds. He will be with them in danger, in difficulty, in perplexity.

J. HUDSON TAYLOR, *God's Fellow Workers*

Rescue Teens Through Prayer - I

Every teenager is under constant pressure from many sources. They are extremely vulnerable to all kinds of evil influences as this is the most difficult physical and emotional time of their lives.

At a time of life when many adults "write them off" as irrational, uncontrollable, moody and unpredictable, God seeks to do a powerful work of drawing them to Himself. Therefore there is a critical need for adult believers to be encouraged and equipped to pray for our youth. With so few godly role models or mentors, teenagers desperately need prayer if they are to grow and mature in Christ.

Teens must have God's power to live victoriously. Just saying "No" is not enough. We need to pray Spirit-led, thoughtful, in-depth prayers for God to protect them before crises develop, as they fight major spiritual battles.

Salvation
In light of the troubled, antagonistic world in which teens live, pray that they will have assurance of their salvation, be fully aware of God's love for them, and not be ashamed to be called Christians.

Spirit-filled
The Lord commands us to be filled with the Holy Spirit (Eph. 5:18). Nothing in the spiritual life is accomplished without His power and infilling. Pray that teens will "be filled with the Spirit" and therefore walk in the Spirit (Gal. 5:16, 25).

Grounded In the Word
It is essential that teens be grounded in the Word of God if they are to mature spiritually. Pray that they will realize that in God's Word there are truths to be believed, promises to be claimed, and commands to be obeyed. Pray that they will apply biblical principles in all areas of their lives, that they

ask God to teach them to value prayer and that they will experience God's power. Pray that they will learn to renew their minds by memorizing the Word and use the Scriptures to check out what is said and suggested by others.

Spiritual Maturity

Pray that as teens receive Christ as their Savior, they will seek guidance and wisdom for their daily walk. Pray that the Holy Spirit will reveal to them all that they have and who they really are in Christ (Galatians 2:20, Romans 6-8), that they will realize that Christ is in them and He is their life and that His calling is to a lifelong process of change, growth and maturity. Pray that they will increasingly be aware that God is all powerful, has all knowledge and is everywhere.

Pray that teens will: 1. Learn to love the Lord with all their heart, soul and mind, and serve and obey Him. 2. Know the Lord as the faithful provider and protector and trust Him with every area of their lives. 3. Grow in worshipping God through praise and thanksgiving.

Enoch walked with God. **Genesis 5:22**

How important it is to us all, day by day, to be living for God, walking in holy friendship with Jesus, leaning on Him as our strength and stay. The only preparation worth anything is that of the knowledge of God, of His Word, and of communion with Him who imparts His grace and strength to those who seek His face.

J. HUDSON TAYLOR, *Fruit Bearing*

Rescue Teens Through Prayer - II

Need for Acceptance

Teens have a strong need to know they are loved for who they are, not for their looks, accomplishments, etc. Pray that their parents, youth leaders, teachers and others will affirm them, that their role models/heroes will be godly and that teens will find their significance, acceptance and security in Christ. Many teens may feel that they have never received love, acceptance and affirmation in their homes, which can bring a sense of hopelessness. Suicide can often seem the only way out. Pray that God will protect them against consideration of suicide and that they will accept and honor their own families no matter what the problems and not compare them to other families.

Self-worth

Many teens have bought Satan's lie that their value comes from how well they succeed in the world and what others think of them ie., physical appearance, performance, status, popularity, etc. Pray they would see themselves as God sees them—holy, dearly loved, accepted, forgiven, new creations in Christ, children of God—not because of how they look but because of who they are in Christ Jesus. Pray they will realize their exalted position in Christ.

Teens are struggling with the whole issue of their identity. Who am I? What is my purpose in life? Am I worth anything? What makes me a valuable person? Pray that instead of being overwhelmed by confusion, they will trust Christ and appropriate all they have in Him. Pray they will realize that God wants to change them through difficult circumstances and not necessarily change the circumstances, and that they will turn to Christ and not to various forms of sin when they suffer traumatic loss. Pray they will know to expect changes, and that in trials and temptations God has not promised an easy road, but He has promised His presence and control in all of life's circumstances.

Success can be the root cause of spiritual problems and lead to selfish pride. Failure can lead to depression. Pray that teens will not let success go to their heads, but give God the glory, that they will take a stand against Satan's effective tools of depression or pride, and that God will set them free from fear of failure, from comparison with others, from being socially unacceptable, or from being thought different.

Peer Pressure

Specific prayer is needed as teens face daily temptations, stresses, peer pressure, and satanic attacks. Pray that they will break from the world's self-centered culture and become Christ centered and will be daily transformed by the renewing of their minds. (Romans 12:1-2). Pray that teens will have mental, emotional, doctrinal, and moral stability. Pray they will realize their love for God is expressed through obedience to Him. (John 14:15, 21-23)

Be not faithless, but believing. John 20:27

Lack of trust is at the root of almost all our sins and all our weaknesses; and how shall we escape from it, but by looking to Him, and observing His faithfulness? The man who holds God's faith will not be reckless or foolhardy, but he will be ready for every emergency.

J. Hudson Taylor, *Great Is Thy Faithfulness*

Rescue Teens Through Prayer - III

Potential

Pray that teens will realize that Jesus calls them not because of who they are, but for what Christ has done and can do through them and that they will decide to do their best in everything and reject a materialistic lifestyle. Pray that they be selective in the music they listen to, will learn to pray for wisdom and will establish a biblical evaluation process. Pray that they will realize that the decision not to study, experimenting with sex or drugs, couch-potato TV watching, pornography, etc., can result in lifelong problems. Pray they will realize life is made up of choices between going God's way or their own way and that they are responsible for their choices, and that God won't reveal His will in a specific situation unless they obey what they already know to be His will.

Leadership

Because today's teens are the next generation of Christian leaders, pray they will learn to be accountable, develop in honesty and integrity, and take care of their bodies, that they will equip themselves for Christian service.

Let me glean and gather after the reapers. Ruth 2:7

Let us all leave the fatherland of the world, or at least become strangers and pilgrims in it. Where the need is greatest let us be found gladly obeying the Master's command. For it is in the harvest field, it is among the reapers, that we shall find Him.

J. HUDSON TAYLOR, *God's Fellow Workers*

Rescue Teens Through Prayer - IV

Forgiving

It costs to forgive, but the cost of not forgiving is much higher. Pray that teens will realize that when they have been hurt by someone, that person will continue to hurt them unless they forgive them, and that in Christ they can be free from the past. Pray that they will admit their own sin against others, ask them for forgiveness, and make restitution if possible. Pray that since God forgives them, they must learn to forgive themselves.

Parents

Many teens come from dysfunctional or abusive homes. It is essential that teens know they are loved by their parents through actions as well as words. Teens don't care how much parents know until they know how much parents care. Pray for parents to speak the truth in love; not lecturing but asking the Lord to give opportunities to instruct when teens are most receptive. If teens do not feel accepted, a sense of insecurity can lead them into rebellious behavior. Pray that parents will realize they can be godly parents only if they are godly persons and godly partners, and that they will exercise grace and patience while holding to God-directed limits to provide acceptance and security for their teens. Pray that parents will realize that hurting teens often react in anger and unacceptable lifestyles, and not take it personally. If teenagers do not have godly parents, pray for godly adult friends and role models to guide them with love and acceptance.

Rebellion

Frequently there is an attitude of "I know it all" and "nobody is going to tell me," which can endanger their lives and their future. Pray against the spirit of rebellion and resistance to authority which is so rampant at this age. Pray that teens will have a spirit of brokenness and humility, that pride will be broken, that they will deal with their sins through repentance. (Ps. 51:7), and that they will have a willingness to see another's viewpoint.

Not by might, nor by power, but by My Spirit, saith the Lord. Zechariah 4:6

Few of us, perhaps, are satisfied with the results of our work, and some may think that if we had more or more costly machinery we would be better. But I feel that it is Divine Power we want, not machinery! Wouldn't we do well to give ourselves to humiliation and prayer for nothing less than to be filled with the Spirit?

J. HUDSON TAYLOR, *God's Fellow Workers*

Rescue Teens Through Prayer - V

Temptation

The god of this world constantly seeks to lure teens away from simple and pure devotion to Christ (2 Cor. 11:3). Pray that they will learn to take every thought captive to the obedience of Christ (2 Cor. 10:3-5) ... and know that God's will is good, acceptable and perfect (Rom. 12:2). They will only know this as they present their bodies (the word "bodies" is key since most of what teens are tempted to do involves their bodies) as a living and holy sacrifice to God and have their lives transformed through the renewing of their minds (Romans 12:1,2). Pray that they will learn that temptation is not sinning unless yielded to, that they will take responsibility for their wrong choices and not blame someone else and that they will realize that through Christ is the only way they can effectively say "No" to temptation. Pray they will learn to use Scripture in resisting temptation and that God will especially guard them from sin that will affect them throughout their lives.

Purity and Personal Standards

As teens look for attention, affection and meaningful relationships, they can so easily fall into Satan's trap and yield to sinful desires and sexual immorality. Pray teens will realize that sex outside of marriage is sin and that there are physical, mental and spiritual prices to pay, often for a lifetime (AIDS, pregnancy, bad memories). Pray that they will be taught healthy sexuality and that they will recognize the sinful fruit of much of TV, movies, videos and debasing music. Pray against Satan as he battles for their minds in all areas of purity. Pray they will be aware their bodies are the temple of the Holy Spirit ... that they will remember they reap what they sow (Gal. 6:7) and that they will fully realize they will have victory over the world, the flesh and the devil as they take the responsibility to say "No," and let Christ live His life through them (Gal. 2:20; Rom. 6).

Consecrate yourselves today to the Lord. Exodus 32:29

Let us trust Him fully. Now if never before, now afresh if often before, let us take Jesus as our Master and Lord, and with unreserved dedication give over to Him ourselves, our possessions, our loved ones, our all. He is infinitely worthy; and He will infinitely make up to us all we give to Him.

J. HUDSON TAYLOR, *Dwelling In Him*

Rescue Teens Through Prayer - VI

Repentance and Sin

Teens need to learn what sin is and how to deal with it victoriously. Sin must be recognized, admitted, confessed and cleansed (1 John 1:9). When not dealt with, sin has disastrous, long-lasting results (Heb. 12:15). Pray that teens will recognize, confess and repent of all known sin, that they will walk in the light with Jesus.

Witnessing to Others

With secular humanism in our education system, hostility to God on campus, and the antagonism of the media, we must pray that our youth will see through all of that and take Christ as their Savior.

Pray for the Lord to raise up many teens to share and live the gospel in this ripe harvest field. Pray that churches and para-church groups will equip young people to be ambassadors for Christ (2 Cor. 5:20), that the Holy Spirit will work in hearts and draw people to Himself, and that teens humble themselves and admit their need for Christ. Pray that after being saved, they will be effectively followed up and make Christ the Lord of their lives.

Personal Relationships

Relationships are vital to the security, development, daily life and future of all teens. Pray they will develop wholesome relationships with their parents, use discernment in choosing their friends, especially those of the opposite sex, and be willing to break off all unhealthy relationships. Pray that they will resist the temptation to date non-Christians.

He that eateth Me, even he shall live by Me. **John 6:57**

Communion with Christ requires our coming to Him. Meditating on His person and His work requires the diligent use of the means of grace, and especially the prayerful reading of His Word. Many fail to abide because they habitually fast instead of feed.

J. HUDSON TAYLOR, *Dwelling In Him*

Rescue Teens Through Prayer - VII

Be Alert

Pray that teens will realize they cannot resist the devil (James 4:4) unless they submit to God. Both must be done to be fully effective ... that they would realize this requires moment-by-moment decisions.

Satan and the Occult

Satan, as the "god of this world," uses the influence of the culture in which we live to draw us away from the Lord. Every young person hungers for spiritual reality and often desires to experience the world of the supernatural. Drugs and alcohol are artificial attempts to find that world, but they open the soul to satanic influences.

Pray against the lure of the occult, secret knowledge, special power and thrilling experiences. Pray against the dark influences of music, videos, magazines, books, movies, and TV that glorify Satan.

Pray that parents will provide strong spiritual defenses for their families ... that teens will learn to exercise their authority as children of God, submit to Him and resist the attacks of the enemy ... that they will choose the truth of God's Word as their defense against the deceptions of Satan.

Pray that they will also remain aware of Satan's threefold strategy: the lust of the flesh (fulfilling our desires outside the will of God); the lust of the eyes (coveting that which God does not allow at a particular time or place); the pride of life (self effort or independence from God) ... that they will put on the whole armor of God. (Eph. 6:10-18)

How can I be sure I am praying effectively for teens?

- Accept responsibility and pray regularly and fervently for the specific needs of the teens the Lord lays on my heart.

- Ask the Holy Spirit for guidance as I pray.

- Pray with the authority I have in Christ, to bind the power of Satan. (Mark 3:27)

- Pray the prayer of faith and claim victory. (1 Cor. 15:57-58.)

- Use Scripture as I pray. (Eph. 1:15-22; 3:16-21, Col. 1:9-14)

If we walk in the light ... the blood of Jesus Christ cleanseth us from all sin. 1 John 1:7

Are all your prayers answered? Does each morning bring you no fear? Is each day a psalm, each night a thanksgiving, sometimes sung in the minor keys—but still sung? Do your visitors feel impressed with the reality of the Kingdom? Or, are there many things, some things, perhaps only one little thing, about which you claim to decide for yourself? Remember that only one such claim dethrones altogether your Lord and Master, so far as lies in your power, no matter how trivial the matter may be.

J. HUDSON TAYLOR, *Fruit Bearing*

Afterword

WHEN it comes to praying for missions, many Christians quite naturally do not know where to begin. Prayer for missions begins with a conviction that prayer really is an effective weapon that counts in the conflict. In practical terms this means that the praying Christian at home is as important as the preaching Christian overseas.

When I stand before a man to explain or proclaim the gospel to him, I have no power in myself or my words to open his eyes to the truth or his heart to Christ. God must prepare his heart and open it, and the power by which He does so is the power of the Spirit, using the words of the preacher and the prayers of the pray-er.

Assuming that you are convinced of the reality and effectiveness of intercessory prayer as a spiritual force, let me suggest some ways in which OMF International can help you to become more involved.

First, there is the prayer calendar, which is available from every OMF office. The easiest tool for involvement, these daily requests can be used in family prayers around the breakfast table. In a month you cover individual items all over East Asia and gradually build up a picture of what is happening.

Second, comes praying for an individual. Each missionary writes a regular prayer letter, which is sent to those who have promised to pray for him. If you do not know any missionary personally, we can help you link up with someone who needs just the support you can give.

Third, there are prayer groups all across the nation. These are small circles of a few individuals who get together regularly to pray for Christ's kingdom. New prayer groups are beginning all the time. If there isn't a group in your area, why not consider starting one. It can begin with just two people. Two housewives meeting every Monday for coffee, two businessmen meeting for a sandwich lunch every Wednesday, or two students in their dormitory at night can accomplish much. OMF can give you the training you need to equip you as a prayer group leader or prayer mobilizer.

Numerous opportunities exist to catch the vision of what God is doing on a global scale. If you are interested in learning more about this exciting ministry, call OMF International. Commitment leads to prayer. Prayer leads to commitment. May I invite you to share in this ministry for Asia today. We never needed you more.

DENIS LANE

ABOUT THE AUTHORS

J Oswald Sanders

J Oswald Sanders was one of the 20th century's most prominent Christian leaders, internationally-known Bible teacher, missionary leader and statesman. He was a prolific author whose public Christian ministry spanned seven decades.

Dr Sanders was a significant figure in the transformation of the China Inland Mission into the Overseas Missionary Fellowship, serving as General Director of the mission from 1954 to 1969. Under his leadership, the mission's ministry expanded from China into eight East Asian countries.

A systematic thinker, Sanders had a way of breaking down complex ideas into understandable segments. His *Effective Faith* (OMF Books) and *Effective Prayer*, excerpted in this volume, are prime examples of the clarity and sharpness of his thought.

He authored over 40 books which have sold more than 2 million copies in 23 different languages. In 1980 Dr Sanders was awarded the Order of the British Empire (OBE) by Her Majesty the Queen. In 1992 he accepted an honorary doctorate in theology from the Bible College of New Zealand. Dr Sanders died in October, 1992 at the age of 90.

J O Fraser

James Otram Fraser began his missionary career in 1908. He was a diligent student of the Chinese language, a gifted Bible teacher, an accomplished musician, and a dedicated man of prayer. He became interested in the mountain tribes in China, and devoted himself to the Lisu, whose spoken language he mastered and reduced to writing for the first time, using a form of script he devised himself.

Fraser tirelessly gave himself to the Lisu, translating two of the Gospels into their language and in later years worked with others to translate the remaining New Testament. He labored without ceasing on their behalf, making extensive journeys along the rugged mountain paths to visit the isolated villages. His love for them won their confidence and endeared him to them. In spite of physical hardship he was always willing to go wherever the voice of the Lord called.

Fraser was an avid personal writer and his journals have yielded a wealth of insights into his life of faith. Drawing extensively upon these journals, his biographer, Geraldine Taylor, crafted the classic biography *Behind the Ranges* (OMF Books), from which the chapter "The Prayer of Faith" which appears in this volume was excerpted. In recent times his daughter, Eileen Fraser Crossman, has compiled a new biography entitled *Mountain Rain* (Shaw Publishers), portraying Fraser's timeless character and enduring faith.

Dr Will Bruce

Wilbert H Bruce is best known for his practical pamphlets on prayer. In all, the pamphlets are approaching the 2 million publication mark, and are being translated into an increasing number of foreign languages. Will joined the Overseas Missionary Fellowship 40 years ago and spent 13 fruitful years in the Philippines as well as many years on the home team as regional director and later as minister-at-large. Dr Bruce and his wife Jean, who are now with the Lord, left for Asia in December of 1959. While in the Philippines, they served in youth evangelism, radio work, literature distribution and training of nationals. He helped found Christ for Greater Manila, now known as Growth Ministries, and was involved in speaking at Bible conferences and evangelistic campaigns.

In May 1993, 42 years after being ordained to the ministry, Will received a Doctor of Divinity degree from Linda Vista Baptist College and Seminary in San Diego, California. His prayer pamphlets include *Why and How to Pray for Missionaries*, *Praying for One Another*, *Saturation Praying*, *O God Revive Us Again*, *Rescue Teens Through Prayer* and *Praying for Missionaries' Children*.

J Hudson Taylor

Hudson Taylor was not only the founder of the China Inland Mission, he was the father of the entire faith mission movement.

From his birth in 1832, Hudson Taylor was fascinated with China. By the age of 21 he had settled his course and was aboard the little clipper ship *Dumfries* bound for Shanghai. Out of deep respect and appreciation for the Chinese culture he adopted Chinese dress in order to minister more effectively.

A physician by training, Taylor poured himself into treating the sick and preaching. Soon a fledgling church was established in Ningpo. However, in eleven of the eighteen provinces there was not a single Protestant missionary. In due time Hudson Taylor's vision of reaching inland China was realized, and the small band of 16 missionaries with whom he began the China Inland Mission in 1865 had swelled to a mighty army of almost 1400, becoming at one point the largest mission in the world.

Constantly busy with endless rounds of speaking engagements, personal visits, correspondence and the operation of the new mission, Taylor still began each morning with prayer. He had a profound influence on the life of the Church. By the time of his death in 1905, many mission agencies had adopted his methods and were seeing unparalleled fruit as a result.

A young Chinese evangelist fittingly expressed the scope of the gift Taylor left the Church in these words: "Dear and venerable pastor, we too are your children. You opened for us the road to heaven. We do not want to bring you back, but to follow you."